COACHING HOCKEY

With

SMALL-AREA GAMES

DAVE CAMERON

HUMAN KINETICS

Library of Congress Cataloging-in-Publication Data

Names: Cameron, Dave, 1980- author.
Title: Coaching hockey with small-area games / Dave Cameron.
Description: First edition. | Champaign, IL : Human Kinetics, [2023]
Identifiers: LCCN 2022024870 (print) | LCCN 2022024871 (ebook) | ISBN
  9781718213791 (paperback) | ISBN 9781718213807 (epub) | ISBN
  9781718213814 (pdf)
Subjects: LCSH: Hockey--Coaching. | Hockey--Training
Classification: LCC GV848.25 .C36 2023 (print) | LCC GV848.25 (ebook) |
  DDC 796.96207/7--dc23
LC record available at https://lccn.loc.gov/2022024870
LC ebook record available at https://lccn.loc.gov/2022024871

ISBN: 978-1-7182-1379-1 (print)

Acquisitions Editor: Diana Vincer; **Developmental Editor:** Anne Hall; **Managing Editor:** Shawn Donnelly; **Copyeditor:** Bob Replinger; **Permissions Manager:** Laurel Mitchell; **Graphic Designer:** Julie L. Denzer; **Cover Designer:** Keri Evans; **Cover Design Specialist:** Susan Rothermel Allen; **Photograph (cover):** filo /DigitalVision Vectors/Getty Images; **Photographs (interior):** © Human Kinetics; **Photo Production Manager:** Jason Allen; **Senior Art Manager:** Kelly Hendren; **Illustrations:** © Human Kinetics; **Printer:** Versa Press

Human Kinetics books are available at special discounts for bulk purchase. Special editions or book excerpts can also be created to specification. For details, contact the Special Sales Manager at Human Kinetics.

Printed in the United States of America   10 9 8 7 6 5 4 3 2 1

The paper in this book is certified under a sustainable forestry program.

Human Kinetics
1607 N. Market Street
Champaign, IL 61820
USA

United States and International
Website: **US.HumanKinetics.com**
Email: info@hkusa.com
Phone: 1-800-747-4457

Canada
Website: **Canada.HumanKinetics.com**
Email: info@hkcanada.com

E8667

Tell us what you think!
Human Kinetics would love to hear what we can do to improve the customer experience. Use this QR code to take our brief survey.

CONTENTS

Game Finder   iv
Foreword   vi
Acknowledgments   viii
Key to Diagrams   ix

CHAPTER 1   Benefits of Small-Area Games 1

CHAPTER 2   Designing Your Own Small-Area Games. . . . 13

CHAPTER 3   Warm-Up Games 21

CHAPTER 4   Offensive and Defensive Games. 47

CHAPTER 5   Specialty Team Games. 85

CHAPTER 6   Transition Games 109

CHAPTER 7   Face-Off Games 133

CHAPTER 8   How to Apply to Game-Like Situations 155

CHAPTER 9   Developing Practice Plans From Drills
to Small-Area Games 165

About the Author   189

GAME FINDER

Game	Difficulty level	Players	Minutes	Primary skill emphasis	Secondary skill emphasis	Page number
CHAPTER 3 WARM-UP GAMES						
Warm-Up Passing	Easy	Full team	6-8	P	St	26
Box Warm-Up	Moderate	Full team	6-8	SA	P	28
1 vs 1 to Dot Line	Easy	Full team	6-8	C	St	30
Neutral-Zone Chaos — Stickhandling	Easy	Full team	6-8	St	SA	32
Keep-Away — Stickhandling	Easy	Full team	6-8	St	SA	34
Three-Zone Scrimmage	Moderate to hard	Full team	9	P	St	36
Neutral-Zone Passing Chaos	Easy	Full team	6-8	P	SA	38
Cross Ice 1 vs 1	Easy	Full team	6-8	St	C	40
2 vs 1 Box Game	Easy	Full team	8-10	P	SA	42
Puck Protection Maze	Easy	Full team	6-8	St	FS	44
CHAPTER 4 OFFENSIVE AND DEFENSIVE GAMES						
Crash the Net	Moderate	Full team	10-12	P	St	56
Net-Front Battle	Moderate	6-8 players with one goalie	8-10	C	P	58
1 vs 1 High and Low	Easy	4 players to a full team (and at least one goalie)	8-10	P	C	60
2 vs 2 Backcheck	Hard	Full team	8-10	C	FS	62
2 vs 2 in Zone	Hard	Full team	8-10	P	C	64
Sideline Game	Easy	Full team	8-10	P	St	66
Neutral-Zone Protect Your Net	Moderate	8-10	8-10	C	SA	68
3 vs 2 Clear the Line	Moderate	Full team	8-10	St	P	70
3 vs 3 High Player in Offensive Zone	Hard	Full team	10-12	P	C	67
2 vs 2 Half Ice — Players Waiting	Hard	Full Team	8-10	FS	P	72
3 vs 2 Forecheck	Hard	Full team	10-12	FS	C	74
1 vs 1, 2 vs 2, 3 vs 3	Easy	Full team	8-10	C	St	76
Add a Player	Moderate	Full team	10-12	P	St	77
Slot Box Game	Easy	Full team	8-10	P	SA	78
Neutral-Zone Two-Puck Game	Moderate	Full team	10-12	P	St	80
1 vs 1 Confined Space	Easy	Full team	8-10	St	C	82
CHAPTER 5 SPECIALTY TEAM GAMES						
End-Zone Power Play	Moderate	Full team	10-12	P	C	90
Nets Back to Back Power Play	Moderate	Full team	10-12	P	C	92

*Skills: BS = backward skating, C = checking, FS = forward skating, P = passing, SA = skating agility, Sh = shooting, and St = stickhandling.

Game	Difficulty level	Players	Minutes	Primary skill emphasis	Secondary skill emphasis	Page number
2 vs 2 Low-to-High Power Play	Moderate to hard	Full team	10-12	P	Sh	94
5 vs 4 Timed Shift	Moderate	Full team	10-12	C	P	96
Power-Play Puck Retrieval	Hard	6-8	6-10	FS	C	98
3 vs 4 Shot Blocking	Moderate to hard	Full team	10-12	C	P	100
2 vs 2 With Plus 1	Hard	Full team	10-12	P	SA	102
Behind Net Passing	Easy	5 players with or without a goalie	6-8	P	SA	104
3 vs 2 Half Zone	Easy	Full team	8-10	P	SA	103
3 vs 2 High	Hard	Full team	8-10	P	St	106
CHAPTER 6 TRANSITION GAMES						
Passing for Points	Moderate	12-18	10-15	P	SA	116
Two Net — Read the Play	Moderate	Full team	10-15	P	SA	118
3 vs 3 Cross Ice	Easy to hard	Full team	10-15	FS	P	120
1 vs 1 With Help Coming	Hard	Full team	10-15	C	St	122
3 vs 3 Angle	Hard	Full team	10-15	SA	C	124
Pass to Coach	Easy	Full team	10-15	P	SA	126
3 vs 3 With Low Player	Hard	Full team	10-15	SA	P	128
Pass to Support	Easy	Small group to full team	8-10	P	SA	115
2 vs 1 in Zone	Hard	Full team	10-12	P	St	130
One Player in Box	Hard	Full team	10-12	SA	P	131
CHAPTER 7 FACE-OFF GAMES						
Face-Off Practice	Easy	Forwards	6-8			139
Edge Battle	Easy	Forwards	6-8			140
Win the Puck	Moderate	Full team	6-8			141
3 vs 3 Face-Off — Offense and Defense	Moderate	Full team	8-10			142
Winner Stays	Moderate	Full team	8-10			144
Face-Off 3 vs 3 — Cross Ice	Moderate	Full team	8-10			145
2 vs 1 Face-Off	Easy	Small group to full team	6-8			146
Speed Draws	Easy	Small group to full team	6-8			148
5 vs 5 Game Simulated	Hard	10 players and a goalie	8-10			150
1 vs 5 Face-Off	Hard	Full team	8-10			152

*Skills: BS = backward skating, C = checking, FS = forward skating, P = passing, SA = skating agility, Sh = shooting, and St = stickhandling.

FOREWORD

I met Dave Cameron, who was a coach in Winnipeg, after I had heard about him from some other players in my area. He had a reputation that was growing, and I was looking to add pieces to my game that would make me a better player. I wasn't looking for a guy who was going to make things easy on me because I played in the NHL; I wanted something different that would challenge me and make we work on different areas of my game. I approached Dave at the end of the 2014 season and let him know that I wanted to get to work right away.

That initial summer that Dave and I started working together was one of the most interesting and humbling summers of my life. Dave showed me things I was good at and, more importantly, showed me things I was not good at, and we worked to correct them. We spent time working on skating, puck skills, shooting (a lot of time on shooting), rims, winger play, and stick position as we developed a general sense of where I could use specific skills in game situations. He set up a plan for me to work through the summer, and I was blown away by the improvement that I made.

After coming off the summer in 2014, I felt more confident in training camp. This improvement led me to have the best two years of my life, with another summer in between them. I was continually getting better and adding new elements to my game. I went from being a fringe NHL player who was not playing very much to being a player who was sought after as an unrestricted free agent and now had 10 contracts to pick from. Each summer, Dave added new sessions like eye position, puck placement, hand–eye coordination, and much more for me to work on and add into my game.

Dave was great at challenging me to work on each of these skills—little things like handling a rim below the goal line and making a play from that spot (on both the forehand and backhand side), handling passes on my backhand, and receiving passes in bad areas around my body and getting them into an area where I could make a play as quick as possible. While we were working on these skill plays, Dave always found a way to work on body positioning and balance, which tied in perfectly. I was able to connect the idea of working on these skills and add them into games to see some success.

As we moved through the off-seasons, I started to add in group training sessions and small-area games like the ones in this book, which allowed me to really use the skills that I had spent hours working on and apply them against other players and in game situations. I noticed that the practices got easier and the games got better. I was able to make quicker decisions and make the right play more often from the work I did with Dave. I really feel like the combination put me ahead of other players who were battling for roster spots because it gave me the best of both sides of things: I had a private coach in Dave who looked out for me and helped with my game, and I also had a coach who was pushing a group of players to get better.

Dave was very good at explaining (and demonstrating at a very high level) the drill we were working on, and he was able to explain exactly why we were working on that particular skill and how it related to a game situation. Seeing the group get better each off-season helped me prepare for training camp and be ready to stand out on day one of each new season.

Over time, I gained a tremendous amount of respect for the way Dave thinks about the game. He was able to recognize little things that I needed to improve (like body position, shoulder checks, stick position, and more) but had never been taught as a full-time NHL hockey player. His ability to take those skills and simplify them into something players can work on together was incredible. Dave has a great feel for players, and his ability to tie skills to practice and lead them into games is truly something special.

I consider Dave not just a coach who worked with me but also a great friend; he was often my first call or text if there was something that I was unsure of about my game. I respect his honesty, because Dave always made me work on things that I was uncomfortable with, which made me much better in the long run.

I went on to play six more seasons in the NHL after working with Dave in private sessions and group sessions. I do not believe that this would have happened if we had not met in 2014. In short, Dave is a fantastic hockey coach, and you stand to learn a lot from him on the following pages.

DALE WEISE
10-Year NHL Player

ACKNOWLEDGMENTS

During a time when work was slow and hockey wasn't being played, I was looking for challenges to get into. I found myself on the radio for Manitoba Moose games, and I found my way into writing a book. The idea of crafting a book was thrown at me, and it was something that interested me but also something I never thought I would face. I wrote down all the things I wanted to talk about and made notes of all the small-area games I used in sessions as a coach. Pretty soon, things started to come together. Over time, my notes began to look like a book.

I would like to thank my wife and daughter for their everlasting support and love and their involvement in my career. I could not have taken on this task without you guys.

Thank you to the people I have worked with at Human Kinetics, who were hugely supportive and critical at the same time. They challenged me to think differently and put my thoughts into words, and they helped me piece my words together.

I am very fortunate. I get to work with all levels of hockey from beginners to NHL players. I get to see the struggle of players learning the game, and the struggle of players not grasping something that they should be able to grasp but can't for some reason. I also get to see the smile on the faces of players who do something for the first time or score a goal using something we worked on. It is this smile—that feeling of "I got it!"—that continues to motivate me to do more as a coach. Thank you to all the players I have worked with over the years who continue to challenge me to be the best coach I can be and help make each player better.

KEY TO DIAGRAMS

X O	Player
X ‖	Player with stick extended
X.	Player with puck
⊗	Player on other team
C	Coach
D	Defensive player
O	Offensive player
G	Goalie
Cr	Center
Ⓒⓡ	Center on other team
W	Winger
Ⓦ	Winger on other team
▲	Cone or tire
- - - - - - - →	Pass
———————→	Player skating
ᴖᴗᴖᴗᴖᴗᴖᴗ	Backward skate
⟨	Net
∴∴∴	Pucks
⟹	Shoot

CHAPTER 1

Benefits of Small-Area Games

Hockey is a unique sport because it quickly changes every shift. Forwards, defensive players, and goalies constantly make decisions about how to manage the situations they are currently in as well as try to think ahead to what will happen next. Practice is a great time not only to work on the necessary skills players need to play the game but also to prepare them to use those skills. Building practice plans to develop skills and then apply them is a useful progression plan because it will help players develop confidence in their abilities and then understand how to use those skills effectively in game situations. Many young players have a good skill base but are unable to bring out those skills in games because they have not yet built up enough confidence. The challenge for coaches is to help players develop their skills to a point where they can freely use them in a game. As coaches, we want to build up the decision-making abilities in players so that they can read the ice, make the right play at the right time, or be in the right spot at the right time. The challenge is that if we rely only on matches to do this, players will not get the feedback quickly enough or will be unable to connect with what the coach is talking about on the bench between shifts. Also, the same situation (or decision) we were trying to explain or correct often does not come up again right away, so the player may forget what was discussed or forget about the play entirely. Practice is the best time to help in the decision-making process because the coach can control what decisions are being made and influence the decision-making process. Drills can be set up with the options you would like to see, and you can be close enough to help the player, vocally, choose the outcome you are looking for. Using drills that allow players different options is a good way to help them understand why they are doing things. By addressing situations in practice and building situations toward games, coaches can start to prepare players for circumstances that will come up. Players will be able to connect learning a skill in a slower practice setting to working in a drill with motion and speed before finally using it in a competitive situation, allowing them to build confidence in their own ability and use the worked-on skill in a game setting.

Small-area games are an effective way to transfer the skills and information that players are working on in practice through drills to a more competitive environment like the one they will see in games. The best results in using small-area games come from connecting the topics directly to something you have worked on in practice or would like to see in a game setting from your team. The ability to teach right away, illustrate points, provide feedback to players, and let them play freely a little bit can lead to accelerated learning from both the individuals and the group.

Research has shown the benefits of small-area games in a variety of sports. Famous soccer players from countries like Brazil have talked about the benefits of their game futsal, which shrinks the field down and confines the players to a smaller space. Growing up playing the smaller modified version of the bigger game soccer helped players develop greater skills with the ball, better understanding of space, quicker ball movement, and quicker decision making. Other sports have also seen the benefits of small-area games to help connect training to game play (Brisbane Central Futsal. Futsal Vs Soccer. www.brisbanecentralfutsal.com/futsal-academy/futsal-vs-soccer).

Small-area games can be beneficial when you relate topics to something that will help the players on your team, but they can be detrimental to development if you use them only to fill time in practice without connecting practice to games. Picking and using small-area games is a challenge because you want to use games that motivate your players to continue to develop.

Small-area games can be useful for a variety of ages. They can jump-start enjoyment of the game for younger players and reinvigorate passion for the game for older players. For young and developing players, small-area games allow more opportunity to play. The players get to move around with lots of skating. The continuous action means that they rarely stand around and lose focus. The movement chasing the puck, backchecking, and working to get up in the play will help players develop their skating skills. The game can be structured with fewer rules so that the kids can focus on the game, not the rules. Because you give the players less tactical instruction, they can focus on simple skills. Young players can learn the individual skills necessary to play the game, like puckhandling and passing. They can build confidence because they will be closer to the play, and weaker players will not feel as if they are left out or way behind (compared with playing the full ice).

Older players can benefit from small-area games because coaches can really start to connect specific areas of practice with more competitive situations. By giving players rules to follow, you force them to think about the situation. The concept of hockey sense can be added to include key elements that will be beneficial to them as they continue to learn about the game. Players can be introduced to topics such as playing off the puck, moving to available space, stick positions, and puck transitions in a setting where the pace matches that of a game. By challenging older players to think, we can start to prepare them for situations they will inevitably see in the game when they have to read and react. By reading and reacting in practice with a coach nearby providing feedback, players will become more successful at reading and reacting in games.

BENEFITS OF SMALL-AREA GAMES AS A TOOL IN PRACTICE

The following list of ideas allows you as the coach to start to think about why you are using small-area games and how you can use them in an effective practice. These ideas are meant to encourage coaches to think about why they are using small-area games rather than running another drill in practice. When you are planning practice, think about what you are trying to get out of it and focus on player development.

Increases Player Engagement

Players will feel that they are involved in the game if the coach manages the game correctly. The coach should control ice time so that it is evenly distributed among the players. If one player stays out longer than they were supposed to in a non-coach-controlled game, the other players will follow their lead and shift length will become unmanageable. Ultimately, the goal for player engagement is not only to have the players playing the game but also, and more important, to connect the skill or concept being worked on to its use in a regular game. This result comes from the players who are not playing but instead watching the game being played and learning from their time on the bench.

Reinforces Team Concept Development

The coach will be able to use games that cover the areas that they would like to see developed by their players. Games can be customized to include topics that your team is struggling with or specific areas that need to be addressed. As a coach, be creative in coming up with games that will benefit your group of players. Not every game will work on what you need. Pick games or put in rules that apply to what you want to see from your group of players or that focus on areas that you addressed during that day's practice.

For example, if a theme for practice is on getting pucks to the net or being first to rebounds, you can add that emphasis into games. Puck possession off a shot is worth 1 point, and a rebound goal is worth 2. So although players are trying to score in the game, they will also be thinking about being first to loose pucks. Adding concepts that players worked on in practice is the best way to come one step closer to making those skills happen in games.

Improves Coach and Player Communication

Small-area games provide many opportunities for the coach to interact with players by reinforcing things they are seeing in the games or just communicating with them in a different way than they can in practice or a regular game. If you can, have an assistant coach spot the pucks or change the lines so that you can interact with the players individually. As the head coach, you can insert exactly what your expectations are from that game. In practice, sometimes things are missed because the coach is watching the drill and not the details of the player. With a team doing the drill, things may slip by and not be corrected. In a game where the space is smaller and players are closer, communication can be quicker and corrections can be made much easier.

Allows Efficient Ice Utilization

For many young teams in minor hockey, practice time may allow use of only half the ice, so the ice surface is already shortened. For older teams who have the full ice sheet, the ice surface can be divided up into space that works best for the games you want to play. By being creative in practice, you can be effective using whatever space you have. What is important is how you use the space based on the number of players you have and the concepts of the games you want to play.

Smaller areas (e.g., games with nets facing each other in the corner) will create games with the following features:

- Less skating
- More stops and starts
- More puck protection
- More shots (closer, tighter plays)
- More rebounds (net-front play)
- Tighter deflections
- Quicker puck movement
- Quicker decisions
- Smaller passing lanes

- Less time and space
- For older groups, more contact

Larger areas (e.g., games with nets in the same zone playing 3 vs 3 cross ice) will create games with these features:

- More skating
- More time and space
- More play off the puck
- More room for vision
- More puck movement
- Larger passing lanes
- More space for plays to develop
- Shots from a great distance
- More deflections from different angles
- More plays off the rush
- More transitional plays from defense to offense

Increases Competitive Aspect in Practice

Concepts like puck possession and defending with the feet are a huge part of hockey, and using games to drive up the competitive aspect in practice is a big part of team development. When you can combine offensive and defensive topics together (no matter which one you are focusing on) and challenge players with competition, you will see the intensity go up in practice. Encourage players to battle within the rules so that you are not working on your penalty kill the next time you get together as a group for practice after a game.

Promotes Decision Making Under Pressure

As the space becomes smaller, the time available to make a decision goes down. Many players struggle with the concept of limited space because they are not used to playing this way. One of the offensive concepts that teams constantly work on is creating space or working into new, available ice. By taking space away from players, we force them into uncomfortable situations. They must react faster, move the puck faster, and make quicker decisions. Players may struggle the first time they play these types of games. The communication aspect from the coach comes in here because players may struggle when receiving feedback that is designed to help them improve. Coaches can let them know that it is OK to have a tough time but also help the struggling players with what they see. This feedback can really help the player see improvement; after a couple of shifts or the next time the game is played, improvement is often noticeable.

Emphasizes Conditioning Instead of Skating

Adding small-area games into practice can help increase the physical conditioning of your players in a game-like setting. With "bag skate" conditioning, players often know the duration of the skate and manage their energy levels for that skate according to the time left in practice. It is difficult for players to go as hard as they can while skating lines. In a small-area game, however, where there is a line skate on the line, players will go as hard as they can to avoid having to do a line skate. By adding a game to the end or start of practice, you can see players start to push the tempo and build up their cardiorespiratory training. A game at the end of practice can prove to be more beneficial than a skate because players will likely push harder to win the game.

By using a situational game rather than skating to build up conditioning, as the coach you can also start to build into the players' heads what a reasonable shift length is for your team and what they should expect during games. This approach is effective when you have players who try to stay out too long in games. You can set up shifts for 15 seconds, 30 seconds, 45 seconds, and 60 seconds and ask players to skate as hard as they can in the game. The quality of the game may not be good for the longer shifts, but players will quickly realize they cannot go that long in a game and be effective for three periods.

Involves More Players

More players are involved in small-area games compared with drills that require longer lines. Players like to feel that they are part of practice, and by constantly moving, they will feel engaged. Situations and games can change to focus on specific areas, and you can change the number of players to make games bigger or smaller. By spending less time in lines, players will also get to push their cardio to be closer to that of a shift in a game.

Includes Goalie Development

Small-area games are valuable for goalie development because situations created by the game can mirror situations that players will see in actual games. This is a great conversation to have with your goalie coach (or an assistant coach if your team does not have one) because you can re-create situations that will come up in the game for the goalies. Gord Woodhall, a goalie coach who works with many high-level goalies and with the National Women's Program for Hockey Canada, states,

> Small-area games are a crucial component for a goaltender's develop-
> ment. An increasingly trending topic in the world of hockey is goalie IQ.
> Goalie IQ consists of several components, which include the goaltender's
> awareness of their ability and position within the context of the game
> situation. The ability for the goaltender to understand their strengths and
> weaknesses allows them to position themselves in the best possible way
> to function in a given situation. In practice drills, when the goaltender
> consistently knows where the release point is or what the objective is for
> the shooter, it is easy to anticipate the save. As a result, this repetitive drill
> allows the goalie a "head start," which allows them to play that situation
> differently than they might in a game. For example, playing with more
> depth on a 2 vs 1 rush drill where the goalie knows the puck carrier has
> to shoot or playing deeper when they know the puck carrier has to pass
> across. These types of drills greatly simplify the goaltender's reads and
> thus remove a substantial amount of environmental stimuli that would
> typically be present in a real game. If only these types of drills are used,
> it limits the opportunity for developing goalie IQ where reads must be
> made at a game pace. This would be similar to a teacher giving a student
> only a part of the material that they will be eventually assessed on.

Gord continued to build on why small-area games are beneficial for goalies by saying,

> Using small-area games provides an environment rich in game-like situa-
> tions where the goalie can identify defensive breakdowns, missed assign-
> ments, and differences in player skill levels. Being immersed in these types
> of situations, goaltenders can learn to identify recurring patterns, making
> players and plays more predictable. With small-area games typically being
> rich in stimuli and unpredictability, goaltenders often find themselves in
> a position (much like a game) where they must abandon their structure if
> they want to make a save. These situations provide a goalie an opportunity
> to explore their abilities, develop their athleticism, and creativity. A final
> benefit of small-area games for goalies is the development of the mental
> side of the game. Small-area games allow for opportunities to play under
> pressure in tight games, deal with bad goals, build off big saves, and ride
> the emotion of the game. Using small-area games effectively for goalies
> allows them to develop the compete mindset and battle mentality that is
> so often sought out by coaches and high-level organizations.

Encourages Thinking About Rules

Players are forced to think about rules for the specific small-area game they are playing. Daniel Tkaczuk, a top-level skills coach who works with the St. Louis Blues organization, spoke on giving rules to players, which showed me the mental benefits of small-area games for players. Daniel and I have worked together with Team Canada for six years, and one of the biggest things I have learned from him regarding small-area games is how the rules are communicated to the players. Daniel said, "Players do not need all the rules of the game; they only need the ones to make the game work. From there players need to be able to figure out how to make the game work better or in their favor" (Tkaczuk, pers. comm). This concept has stuck with me, and I have used it every single time we use a small-area game. In a net-front rebound game, I use the phrase "Touch the nearest boards" to have a new puck come to the front of the net. Right away players assume they must touch the boards on the side wall and come back to the front of the net. At some point, one player will figure out that the "nearest board" is behind the net, and they will get back to the front of the net quicker.

Another example of this is a neutral-zone 2 vs 2 drill (nets at the blue line) I use in which players must score two goals in one shift to get a point for their team. All I tell the players is that each player must touch the puck before they score each goal. At some point the players will figure out that they can play defense against the other team after one player touches the puck. The game is one of my favorites because players must read when to play defense and when to play offense. The game can be 2 vs 0 (two offensive players and a goalie) in both ends, 2 vs 1 in one end and 1 vs 0 in the other, or two 1 vs 1 games. The best part of the game is that the scenarios are always changing based on where the puck is.

By giving players rules for the game, you make them think about how they can best use those rules while also allowing them to be creative and think about what else they can do around the rules that were given. Often, when I use small-area games, players ask, "Can we do that?" and my reaction is, "I did not say you could not do that," which typically leads to greater effort to push the rules.

Addresses Individual Skills

Games can be chosen to allow players to continue to work on a variety of skills that are relevant to them as individuals and that will help in their development. Games can include skating skills, puck skills, passing skills, and shooting skills. Focusing on those key areas can expose players to using their skills more in a competitive environment.

Individual Skating Skills

Players will have to work on skating topics that are directly transferable to the game. When players are having trouble with skating concepts in practice or in small-area games, that should tell you that you need to work on those topics in practice or have the players' skating coach work on them. Skating topics include the following:

- Balance
- Ability to react
- Forward acceleration
- One-foot edge development (inside or outside edge)
- Two-foot edge development (two edges working together, e.g., tight turn with inside edge on one foot and outside on the other or 10 and 2 turn with inside edge on both feet)
- Deceptive skating—a topic I call "creating unpredictable paths," in which the skater makes an opponent think they are doing something they are not through their skating
- Stops and starts
- Lateral movement (both offensively and defensively)
- Transition skating—from both backward to forward and forward to backward

Individual Puck Skills

Building players' abilities with the puck gives them the confidence to want the puck in the game. Developing a wide range of puck skills will come from practice because studies have shown that players just do not have the puck enough in games to lead to continued development. Individual puck skills include the following:

- **Stickhandling**—more touches of the puck in competitive situations to expand their existing skill set. This skill would eventually lead to topics such as puck protection and fakes.
- **Passing**—building on more touches to expand to more movement of the puck.
- **Pass receiving**—as the puck moves more, players will get more chances to receive the pass. Even defensively, players can work to intercept the pass, which would still involve receiving the puck.
- **Shooting**—having a variety of shots available to the player based on the situation in the small-area game. Topics like quick release or backhand shots can be included in the rules of the game by having

them be worth an additional point to ensure that players work on them in the game.

- **Symmetry skills**—this topic includes stickhandling, passing, and shooting whereby players can make plays with confidence on both their forehand side and backhand side. I am not encouraging rink-wide backhand saucer passes, but I am encouraging players to make plays as they see them. Think about a player in the offensive zone below the goal line with the puck on their backhand. The player sees an open teammate in the slot and moves the puck to create an offensive chance (maybe a goal). If the passer takes the time to adjust the puck to their forehand, the passing lane may close or the open player may no longer be available. Players should be ready to move the puck when they are supposed to, not when they have to.

Individual Checking Skills

Checking is partly a combination of skating ability and strength, and partly about a player's willingness to engage physically against another player. This action does not have to include body checking (although it can), but players need confidence in their ability to get close to an opponent and attempt to get the puck off the opponent's stick. Individual checking skills include the following:

- **Angling**—good angles come from good skating and confidence in edges and spatial awareness. A player must be able to adjust to an opponent's speed and take the necessary ice to steer them where they want them to go. Eventually, the player wants to run the opponent out of room with the stick to the puck and the body to their body.

- **Strength on skates**—having confidence in skating to be strong on the skates when the time to battle for the puck comes up either offensively or defensively.

- **Stick position**—keeping in mind the defensive stick mentioned earlier, this idea can also include using one hand on the stick to become bigger or two hands on the stick to be stronger. Players need to understand both options and where and when to use each of them to be effective checkers.

- **Reaction to realistic movements**—this point relates to removing limits from drills. In practice, coaches often say, "The player must drive wide and cannot cut back to the middle." This directive allows the checker to adjust their angle, knowing that the player cannot cut back. When movement is not restricted in the small-area game, the checker must react to the situation and can learn from how players move in the available space.

- **Controlling players' positions**—working to be in a good checking position all the time and not getting beat back to the net or to available space.

When planning to use small-area games, be mindful of factors that will lead to that game being beneficial for your group of players. Stay away from using a small-area game just to use a small-area game. Be aware of factors like the age of your players, the skill level of your group, the time of the season, and the energy level required by the schedule. Try to put players in situations that will allow them to grow as players or work on something specific. The timing of specific games can be helpful in development, and the coach controls the use of specific games. Keep in mind that as more players are added to games, less space is available, so choose your games wisely to focus on specific areas that you want to develop. If players are not yet comfortable under pressure, give them more space to work in by either choosing a bigger game or using the ice to add more games with more space. Until you have worked on and seen improvement in topics like puck protection, be careful not to put players in situations where they will simply throw the puck away under pressure.

Small-area games are most effective when they connect to your team and lead to areas that you want to improve as a group.

CHAPTER 2

Designing Your Own Small-Area Games

The job of the coach in any sport is to help athletes develop in a way that allows them to see success. In hockey, younger athletes practice far more than they play matches, so the coach must create a practice environment that helps players develop a love for the game. The young players' love for the game will come from interacting with their friends, working on developing their skills on the ice, and playing games in practice. The coach chooses the games that the players play in practice to help them prepare for what will come at them in a game situation. The coach can always choose different games based on what is happening at that time of the season or what the group needs to be working on. As the coach, you get to identify the strengths and weaknesses of the players and pick games that suit the skill set of your group. For example, if you have a group of young players who are having trouble with skating, try to reduce the space that they need to cover so that they can feel as if they are more a part of the game. The focus of that game will be more on puck control, passing, and shooting rather than skating to chase the puck. As players develop more skating skills, you can open up the size of the game a little more.

CREATING GAMES FOR YOUNGER ATHLETES

By accurately identifying the skill level of the group, the coach can pick games that allow the players to continually develop in all areas. Managing a practice and picking or creating games that fit into your plan and work for your team is a skill that comes with experience and having some feel for your group. Here are some important areas to identify with your group:

- Keep games enjoyable by setting up an environment where players enjoy playing. Your enthusiasm when players make good passes or plays is important here.
- Focus on introductory skills with games that encourage passing and puck support. Focus on simple skills of puck possession through stickhandling and passing. Teach players about moving to available ice and working together to move down the ice.
- Choose a game that uses skills that you worked on in practice. Progressions in practice can really help develop skills. By using skills in a situation that simulates a game, players gain confidence in their abilities.
- Keep shifts short so that everyone is involved in the game and so that you can introduce the idea of changing lines. Players will learn to work hard for their time in the game and rest when they are not playing.
- Have coaches be continually interacting with the players who are waiting. Use this time to teach and show players things before they go out and play. Players will remain engaged in sessions without losing interest in the drills.
- Use the ice that is available by splitting up when you can.

As players become stronger, the games you choose to play can be specific to certain parts of the game. Using small-area games in practice helps players connect the dots from practice to games. The competitive aspect of the games will create some physicality that resembles a game, which will help prepare players to make decisions quicker and under pressure. By putting players in these situations more often, players can learn what they need to do to be more successful.

CREATING GAMES FOR OLDER ATHLETES

As players get older, the games that you use in practice may become different because of the improvement of skills and the increase in rules. Older players may need to be challenged more than younger players who were starting with basic skill development. Older players can focus on game situations and the application of skills to those game situations. The following list identifies some topics to think about:

- Focus on the needs of the group from the games you have played and areas that you would like to see improvements in. These can be built up through practice and then used in a game to allow players to see the importance of the situation.

- Be specific in what you are hoping to see. For example, when I want to work on deflections, I put a value on deflection goals that is double the value of a regular goal. This rule encourages players to work on deflection situations in the small-area game. Extra excitement always results when a player scores in a way that has a higher point value.

- Re-create situations that you want to develop in your game. Think about situations like winning board battles or winning net-front battles and then add those situations into games so that they become the focus of the game. Board battles can be added to games by moving the nets to the boards and shrinking the area. As the coach, you can add dimensions to the game that include support players both offensively or defensively, or you can simply play the game straight up with the same number of players in the small zone. If you want to focus on creating offense in front of the net, games that are between the hash marks are great for creating net-front battles. Offensively, you want to encourage players to get to free pucks and think about position before possession. Defensively, having players box out and make it difficult for opponents to stand in front can be a focus. These drills always encourage battling for space and loose pucks. Playing below the goal line is a popular topic now for extending shifts in the offensive zone. This focus is a great concept for a small-area game, and it is helpful for the goaltender as well because it re-creates a situation that will come up in the game where the goalie must identify the options and scoring threats in a rapidly changing situation. Down low, players will have to handle pucks on the wall, battle, and make plays to the slot, while the offensive players in the slot must battle to find available ice and be available at the right time when the passer is ready to pass.

ADDING IN CHANGES TO GAMES

When developing games for your players, be creative. Work to see things in practice or games that you can build on with your group and work to find ways to keep them engaged. Small-area games lose their effectiveness if you continually play the same game with the same rules. Players eventually become disengaged in the game and simply go through the motions.

One of the most effective changes I have seen to a simple 3 vs 3 cross-ice game was to take a game and make it a game to 1 goal. This meant that every time a team got scored on, they had to skate a down-and-back (including the goalie). The intensity and involvement from everybody went through the roof, and I could not believe the tempo of the game compared with a regular 3 vs 3 game. The change in this game was implemented leading up to an NHL season and was suggested by a player to add some conditioning to the end of practice. This variation was easily the best game of 3 vs 3 cross ice I have ever seen. I continually use this change to keep the intensity high during a game of 3 vs 3, and I often change the rules to have games to 2 or 3 and have players skating to make up the difference in the score. For example, if a team loses 3-0, they have to skate three full lengths; if they lose 3-2, they have to skate one length. This rule keeps the engagement from the team that is losing because they will not want to skate as much. When creating your own games, you need to consider several key areas.

How Many Players Are Participating in the Practice or Small-Area Game?

The number of players in the game will dictate several factors in the practice and the setup. First, it will determine how much space is needed and whether can you use both ends for the same game (with one goalie in each end). Second, it will determine the shift length. Will players change on their own, or does the shift in the game need to be controlled by a whistle? We always want the game to allow players to see success in the areas they are working on. Having them too tired to play a full-ice game doesn't work, so you may choose to shorten the distance and change the game based on the number of players participating.

What Do You Want to Get From the Game?

To maximize the results that come out of practice, use your practice planning to help determine what game you want to play. Players are constantly wanting to get better and learn from situations, so help them learn by exposing them to situations where they must use something they worked on previously in practice. By forcing them to bring those older topics back out, you are helping them continue to work on those skills.

What Is the Energy Level of the Players?

The energy level of your players will differ from day to day. As a coach, on some days you will need to use a small-area game for longer (or shorter) than you initially planned. If players are exhausted, having them play a game in both ends with small numbers may not be the best idea. Learn how the players are feeling through communicating with the group in practice and work to use their energy in the games.

What Is the Practice Layout Like?

If you start with a game, the players will get energized quickly and you will need to keep that energy going. Starting with a game and then trying to slow down and teach while players stand still will be difficult. When I plan practice to work on power skating, we do not shoot pucks before we teach. I want players to build up to using pucks in the practice instead of starting with them.

Do You Have Two Goalies?

If you do have two goalies, try to play a game in which both goalies are in the game and involved. If you have only one goalie, try to play a game that uses a pass to change possession instead of having one team shoot on an empty net while the other shoots on a goalie. This kind of game will be beneficial for both teams and the goalie will receive a lot of shots.

What Is the Skill Level of the Group?

Be able to adjust the games you like to use to meet the skill level of the group you are on the ice with. You want them to play the game to a good level but also challenge them to expand their existing skill set. Challenging them beyond their existing skill set can frustrate players and cause them to lose interest in the small-area game. By identifying what they can do and where they are with their skill sets, you can implement those areas into the game to help them build confidence in both their own abilities and the abilities of the group.

Ways to Make Games Easier

- Simplify rules.
- Have one net for each team.
- Whistle to line change.
- Adjust space based on skating requirements of the game (more space means more skating and more time for players to make decisions).

Ways to Make Games More Difficult

- Change or modify rules.
- Add details to the game to work on something specific.
- Have transitions in the game to transition from defense to offense.

- Have players change on their own with appropriate shift length (not recommended if you have a big group of players).
- Adjust space based on game requirements (less space will result in more physical engagement and quicker decision making).

Do You Have Enough Coaches for What You Want to Run?

To ensure player development, you need at least one coach running each end. This setup allows you to control the way you want the game to be played. The game that is used should benefit the players. The coach who is with each group should be able to monitor shift length and tell players to change as well as spot pucks into the game. The coach can also communicate with the group to ensure that players are learning as they play the game.

What Rules Need to Be Given to the Players to Allow Them to Play?

Come up with a set of rules that allows your game to function smoothly. How you communicate your rules will determine the success of the game, especially early on in the game. Come up with a set of rules that is simple to follow and challenges players to think about what is happening.

TEAM CANADA CAMP

For the past several years at the U17 Team Canada Summer Development Camp, a group of skills coaches was given the task of planning a 90-minute small-area games session for their respective teams that worked to accomplish several factors in the development of players. Because this session was for the best players in the country, we planned it so that specific areas of focus tied into areas of the team game that were important to the head coach. We tried to plan small-area games that allowed the players to be physical and engage in battles while not crossing the line and taking penalties. We drew a line in the sand on this topic so that if we saw players getting too close to the edge, we could either address it with the group or switch the game. As a coaching staff we tried to identify smaller areas of the game that were important, and we took those concepts and added them into small-area games. We included topics like face-offs to stress the importance of winning the face-off as a group rather than just relying on the center to win every draw. We included multiple games with battles and angling because we knew that some of the other countries that we would play at the tournament would be great skaters. We challenged players to work in small areas to force them to go to specific spots, and we put them in more open ice (bigger areas) to help them to learn to skate with speed to take away ice. We also identified the importance of the specialty teams, so we dedicated games and time to power-play and penalty-kill scenarios where we could watch offensive concepts such as puck possession, puck support, passing, shooting, and ability to win 50-50 pucks. Defensively, we watched for topics like skating, stick position, shot blocking, and willingness to battle. Every minute of the 90-minute ice time was managed to ensure the following:

1. Players were engaged in a game.
2. Communication from coaches was constant to all players. Each game had one coach running the game and other coaches interacting. The coach running the game oversaw that station.
3. Ice was divided for every game to maximize the movement of players. Players rotated from station to station and played multiple games in their 90 minutes of ice time.
4. Players understood the value of each game they were playing and how it connected to the bigger picture of the team game.
5. Players were never allowed to push beyond the acceptable limit of physicality.
6. Energy levels were managed to control the practice so that players got a good, physically active workout.

CREATE A GAME FOR YOUR GROUP

The concept of creating a small-area game for your team revolves around the idea of what your team needs to get better at. If you build from that thought with each practice to include drills and games, your players will be able to work through your plans to develop your team. Adding skills to focus on in practice and in small-area games is an effective way to help players focus on those skills and see how they relate to the game. By giving the players an opportunity to see success through a game that allows them to use their skill set, you are helping them build confidence in their own abilities. When they trust their own abilities, they will not throw the puck away but rather protect it so that they can make a play to someone else. By choosing a game that matches your players' skill set, you are encouraging them to develop their abilities. By choosing a game that is above their skill set, you are challenging them to push to the next level. But this approach can be risky if your players are not ready for the challenge. Expect the quality of this game to be lower because players are working to figure out the game instead of focusing on their play within the game. This level of game can be beneficial if you have time in another practice to come back to it.

When you come back to the game for a second time, you should see some development from the first time the group played it.

By choosing a game that is below your players' skill level, you should expect them to play the game at a high level because they can focus on the game, not the rules. Using a simple game and having players execute at a high level is a good way to build confidence. Rules can be simple, and the pace should be high in this type of game. As the game is played, the expectation is that some of the skills that were worked on will start to show up in games. Players may score a different way or make simple passes more often. Encourage players to do this kind of thing in a simple game so that they understand you are trying to make the game easier for them, not harder.

CHAPTER 3

Warm-Up Games

Warm-up games are useful when the practice to follow has lot of pucks and puck drills. These games get players invested in the practice early and allow numerous touches of the puck. Warm-up games are also beneficial because they will quickly increase the energy level in practice and promote early involvement from everyone.

Coming to practice with a plan is the key to making sure that you maximize time on the ice to build what you want to build or work on what you want to work on during that practice. Having a plan will allow you to accomplish your objectives in that window of time. On days when players are not feeling great or are tired, playing a game early in practice can break them out of that shell and quickly increase their energy level.

COACHING TIP

Using a warm-up game before your drills may not always be the best choice. An example would be a day when you are working on power skating or another skill that requires a lot of detail when teaching. On such days, the focus from players is important. Having them fully energized and then slowing them down can disrupt their focus. If you need players' attention after the game, be careful about how you start practice. A game should lead into something that challenges them to take the next step in practice and builds on the energy created from the game.

BENEFITS OF WARM-UP GAMES

Using a game to start practice is a good way to challenge players to come ready to work. The game at the start of practice creates a setting like a match, and players must use their time in the dressing room leading up to practice to get ready. They have no time to waste, so they must be ready to play at the start of the game, as well as at the start of the practice. You can create a match-type feeling that motivates players to be ready to execute at the start of the training session. Doing this periodically throughout the season can keep players ready at the start of practice and maximize the time spent building your team in practice.

Other benefits of warm-up small-area games include the following:

- Gets players engaged early in practice
- Forces players to focus on the start of practice to maximize their time in the session
- Can create a game-type feeling that players must be ready for
- Involves everyone early in practice
- Creates energy and atmosphere early in practice
- Encourages communication early in practice
- Forces players to think and make decisions early in practice

WORKING WITH YOUR GOALIES

One thing to think about as you add small-area games to the beginning of practice is that the goalies may not have had their normal warm-up unless they were on the ice before practice. This is something to think about as you get into the season as a coach and are concerned about the safety of players. If goalies have not warmed up with movement and shots, using them in a small-area game could be a challenge for them and something that you may want to avoid. If they have been on the ice with their goalie coach a while before practice and have seen shots and moved around the crease, then you can add them to the game at the start of practice without fear of their being injured. Many games can be played that involve just the skaters and allow the goalies to warm up either on their own or with a coach or shooter at the start of practice.

As a coach, when you are having players play games at the start of practice that do not include goalies, a good idea is to focus on a skill that allows players to take something from a previous practice and continue to work on it under more pressure and in game situations. Topics to focus on and situations can change, but the key part to playing a small-area game at the start of practice is that players are using something you have worked on before and taking something away that they can use later (or in a game).

WARM-UP SMALL-AREA GAMES

There is a fine line between small-area games and drills in the warm-up because coaches often want to use a variety of activities to start practice. I often use games as a way to implement something from the current practice (or a different practice) that my team has worked on before and drills to work on something either again or for the first time.

By starting the practice with a game, you can quickly get players on board with the idea that they must be ready to go at the start of practice. This approach will help you get players ready for the start of their games by coming out and playing their best without wasting the first 10 minutes of the game while they ease into it. With most practices being 60 minutes in length, we want to maximize the time by having players do something constructive that will help them build and keep building in their games. Creating an environment where players feel safe and OK to fail is important, because without failing or losing the puck, they might not develop in the area that you are working on. Taking the time to work on skills and then using the skills in a situation (either at the start or end of practice) can allow players to grow their skills before they get to the game. The best way to have skills transfer from practice to game is to have players work on skills, then use their skills, then use their skills against competition, and finally carry their skills into the game.

When players come to practice and enjoy their time on the ice working on various things, they will want to come back and do more. When working on practice plans and building an environment for their team to see success, coaches should ask themselves this question: "Did players enjoy their time in the process of getting better?" Players can be challenged and pushed, but nowadays they want to know why they are doing things and how those things will help them improve as players. When you have answers for the players, you are able to connect better to what they are looking for in their development and can tie that purpose into the team's development.

Using games in the warm-up is a way to challenge players to use their individual skills and focus on what they have worked on previously to execute at the start of a new session. When players can identify what they are working on, they will recognize that you are organized as a coach and have their development on your mind when you are planning practice. The following types of games can be used for warm-ups.

Skating Games

Skating games can be effective after players have worked on their skating without the idea of racing to go faster. Keep in mind that with every game that includes skating, some players will struggle a bit or perhaps feel the pressure of not wanting to let the team down, especially at a young age when they are building up their skating. Skating games can include a variety of topics and can challenge players to work on several different areas of their skating, depending on the space or area that the game is played in. Bigger spaces mean more speed, and smaller spaces mean that players must work more on their footwork in confined space. By changing the skating game that your players are working on, you can start to build well-rounded skaters. Having players react to the space that is provided will allow game-like movements to occur more freely than in drills.

Stickhandling Games

These games require players to get their hands on the puck early in practice and handle the puck with their eyes up when they must make decisions. Topics to start your practice can include puck protection, adding width, avoiding other players, and many others. This type of game can be a good follow-up to a day when players ended a practice with puckhandling. This sequence brings them quickly back to what they had worked on and allows you to push your players beyond where they were. Players can work by themselves, in partners working on puck protection, or in the group doing several different things to work on their stickhandling. Neutral-Zone Chaos—Stickhandling (page 32) is a good way to help players work on stickhandling while keeping their eyes up and working around other players. This game can quickly turn into a game of keep-away, which will help players work on puck protection, adding width, moving away from defenders, and working to find available ice.

Passing Games

Passing games help players see the importance of passing and pass receiving in a game setting. Having players pass the puck and move to get open when they do not have the puck allows them to start to understand that they must be open to get the puck back. Passing games are good at the start of practice because they give players the idea that they must pass the puck quickly when the lane is available, before it gets closed. They can carry this idea into the rest of practice, and it can flow smoothly into your next set of drills.

Shooting Games

Shooting games are hard unless you have a good number of nets on the ice and can work on shooting at the start of the day. I like to use shooting as a warm-up because players can stand in the slot and shoot a lot of pucks quickly. Having multiple nets on the ice for the session allows more players to shoot and work on specific things within their shot. Shooting games can include accuracy games or challenges that force players to shoot to specific areas you are calling out before each player starts shooting. With multiple nets on the ice, you can have three or four players at each net working on shooting and passing pucks to the shooter. With lots of nets and lots of shooters, you need lots of pucks. If you do not have enough pucks, there will be more standing around waiting for pucks than there will be shooting. Shooting games are the least effective type of warm-up game for building specific skills.

WARM-UP PASSING

Level of Difficulty

Easy

Minutes

6-8

Players

Full team. (Note: When I say "full team" in these game descriptions, I mean either a full team or a full group.)

Objectives

To get players moving early in practice with lots of puck touches, movement, and communication.

Setup

Players grab a partner and stand roughly the width of a face-off circle apart. Each set of players needs one puck, and players spread out all over the ice. Space can be left for the goalie to get warmed up or work with their goalie coach.

Procedure

Players start passing the puck back and forth, making sure that passes are on the tape and received when the pass hits their stick. As players are passing the puck, the coach blows the whistle to signal players to go into a puck protection situation in a confined space where they play 1 vs 1 for a short time. One player works to protect the puck, while the other player tries to steal it. On the next whistle, the players without the puck must find a new partner and continue passing. Keep in mind that half the group will be moving to find a new partner, so there could be some confusion. This sequence continues for a couple reps of passing, puck protection, and switching.

Coaching Tips

- Communication is key on the switches because players will have to sort out a new partner. This game is useful in helping players get to know each other at the start of the season because you can ask players to call their teammates by name.
- If you have an odd number of players, a coach can jump in to even out the group so that everyone has a partner.

Variations

When partners change, the type of pass changes. Here are some examples:

- Forehand tape to tape.
- Forehand pass to backhand reception—players handle the puck when they receive it by pulling the puck across their body.
- Backhand pass to forehand reception—players handle the puck when they receive it by pulling the puck across their body the other way.
- One touch—players make quick passes without stopping the pass.
- Spin after receiving the pass—players lose eye contact and then must look before they pass. This variation gets more movement from players because they can spin either way, whichever side they get the pass on.
- Saucer passes—players elevate the puck in their pass back to their partner.
- Pass and move—players move in a small space while facing their partner the whole time, and they must pass in motion in different directions (forward, backward, sliding laterally) while seeing where their partner is.

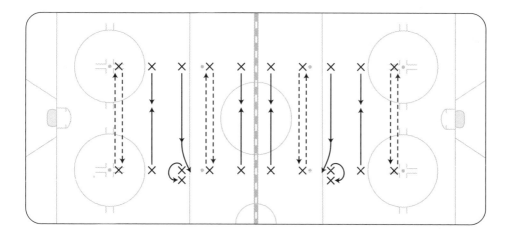

BOX WARM-UP

Level of Difficulty
Moderate

Minutes
6-8

Players
Full team

Objectives
To have players react to where another player goes and eventually work to take their puck away from them.

Setup
Working off the half wall, set up a box of tires (or cones) in each end and one in the neutral zone. Divide players equally among the three areas.

Procedure
On the whistle, two players leave at the same time, both carrying a puck. The first player moves from tire to tire, and the only rule is that they cannot go around the outside to go past each tire once. The second player must react to where they go and work to follow the first player as closely as possible.

Coaching Tip
- Encourage players to be creative in how they move through the four tires. They should be trying to lose the second player, who will be following closely.

Variation
- After players have done this a couple of times, you can turn the second player into a chaser of the first player. The chaser must follow the first player's feet exactly, meaning that they must go around every tire that the puck carrier goes around. The chaser's job is to break up possession of the puck from the first player. The chaser can extend their stick around a tire, so the puck carrier must remember this when moving around and protect the puck from being knocked away.

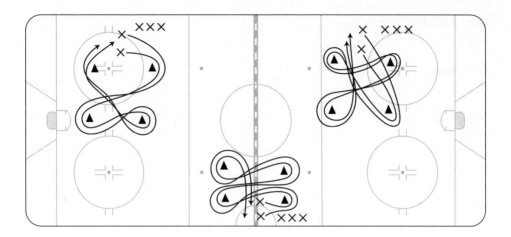

1 VS 1 TO DOT LINE

Level of Difficulty
Easy

Minutes
6-8

Players
Full team

Objectives
Offensively, to get the puck off the wall and to the dot, and defensively, to keep the player against the wall where they can get their stick to the puck.

Setup
Players divide up and space themselves around the ice so that they can work against the wall without interfering with the game beside them. Groups of two or three players should be working all around the ice.

Procedure
On the whistle the defensive player spots a puck against the wall for the offensive player to try to get off the wall to the dot line. The defensive player works to keep the offensive player contained and in a spot where they are limited in their options with the puck. Defensively, the player works to get their stick to the puck and knock the puck away from the offensive player.

Coaching Tips
- Encourage the defensive player to take away time and space quickly and work to have the offensive player keep their back to the defensive player.
- Offensively, the player works to protect the puck and gain shoulder position on the defensive player.

Variation
- After players have done this once or twice, you can add a third player, who is a support option to pass the puck to. The offensive player looks to move the puck to support off the wall. If a successful pass is made to that support player, they must pass the puck right back to the wall for the offensive player to work again.

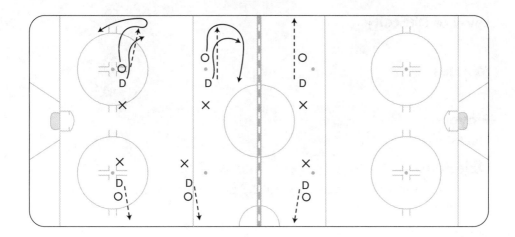

NEUTRAL-ZONE CHAOS—STICKHANDLING

Level of Difficulty

Easy

Minutes

6-8

Players

Full team

Objectives

To develop players' confidence with the puck while working around other players.

Setup

Divide the group into two groups. One group skates with a puck, and one group stands still with their sticks extended.

Procedure

All players in the moving group move around the neutral zone on the whistle, working around other players, who are standing still. The players who are standing still are not trying to get the puck. Have players go for roughly 15 to 25 seconds and then switch the groups. The group that is skating works around the nonskating group and can stickhandle under their stick, through their feet, or around their stick. The puckhandlers must also be aware of each other in the drill because more players are moving around the group.

Coaching Tips

- Encourage players to move at a pace that feels comfortable to them. Challenge players to go faster as they get the hang of where players are and the space that is available.
- Remember to switch groups. This activity works best when the groups can go more than once each so that you can see improvement.

Variations

- After players have gone a couple of times, you can add passing, which is a great communication warm-up. Have players pass the puck to a player who is standing still and then move to get it back. They do not have to move toward the player with their puck but instead should move to available ice where they can get the puck back.

- Next, have the puck carrier pass the puck to a player who is standing still and then get a pass back from a different player. This activity starts to have players work on moving to get open for a puck and communicating. Players may miss some passes in this option or pass the puck to someone who already has a puck, so they must be aware of what is happening around them and who else is passing. Spatial awareness is key in this drill because players must also be able to receive a pass back after they give their puck to a player who is standing still.

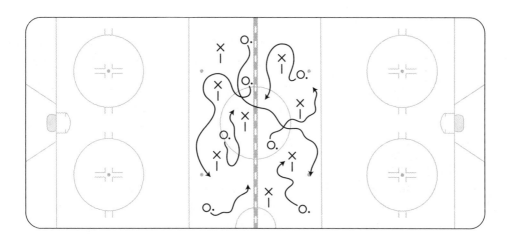

KEEP-AWAY—STICKHANDLING

Level of Difficulty
Easy

Minutes
6-8

Players
Full team

Objectives
To develop players' confidence with keeping the puck away from others while still trying to knock the puck off other players' sticks.

Setup
Players are all in the neutral zone (between either the blue lines or between the red line and blue line) with a puck.

Procedure
Players move around until they hear the whistle. On the whistle, players work around other players while each of them tries to knock the puck off their team-mates' sticks and over one of the lines in the neutral zone. If they can knock another player's puck off their stick and over the line, that player is out and waits at the line that their puck went over. They can reach in and try to take someone else's puck from the spot where they are standing. Players go until one player remains and then play again.

Coaching Tips
- This drill is a good follow-up to Neutral-Zone Chaos—Stickhandling because it has all the players in the neutral zone working on puckhandling.
- Encourage players to have their eyes up and react quickly into available ice. Players may need to protect the puck with their body or their skating to move through pressure.

Variations

- Players can work with a partner and have one puck between the two of them. Players must recognize when they can go work to knock someone else's puck away and when they need to protect their own puck in supporting their teammate. Teams of two can pass between themselves and work to avoid the other checkers in the game.

- This game can also start with three players without pucks, who must try to check players. This option keeps everyone playing at all times because no players are eliminated. After one of these players steals a puck, the player who lost it becomes one of the three who is working to steal someone else's puck.

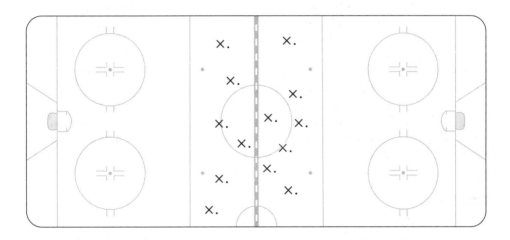

THREE-ZONE SCRIMMAGE

Level of Difficulty
Moderate to hard

Minutes
9

Players
Full team

Objectives
To work on puck movement and communication to start a practice.

Setup
Players are split up into two teams, each team is split up into the three zones, and an equal number of players are in each of the three zones. A time is set so that players have an equal length of time in each of the three zones—defensive, neutral, and offensive (e.g., three minutes in each zone). Two pucks can be used in the game, and each puck provides a separate game. The rule for scoring is that the goalie must be looking at a player's puck before they can score. One team goes one way, and the other team goes the other way. The puck must be passed from the defensive zone to the neutral zone to the offensive zone unless it is turned over by the opposing team; it can then be advanced by one zone or kept in the offensive zone. Passes cannot be made from the defensive zone to the offensive zone, skipping the neutral zone.

Procedure
At the start of the game, a face-off with two pucks occurs. The game is played with players in their respective zones working to get the puck moved up the ice through puck support and puck movement. With each shift being three minutes long, players must move to support the puck and know what they are going to do with it when they get it. A player with the puck in the defensive zone must pass to a player in the neutral zone, who then passes to a player in the offensive zone; the other team works to do the same thing the other way. When the three minutes is up, the players rotate to a new zone and a new three-minute period starts on the clock.

Coaching Tip
- This game allows many things to be worked on, but you must ensure that all players are engaged. With two pucks players almost have to be engaged around the puck or working to get open to get a pass. Players should constantly be scanning the ice to see who is open and who is near them.

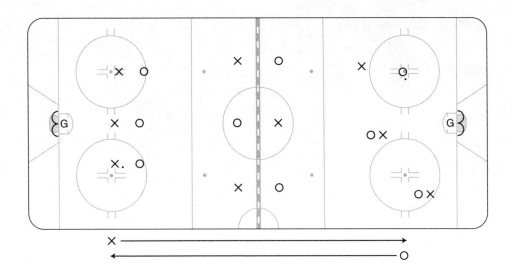

NEUTRAL-ZONE PASSING CHAOS

Level of Difficulty
Easy

Minutes
6-8

Players
Full team

Objectives
To work on passing under pressure while other players are moving around to check and get open.

Setup
Divide players into two teams. The groups are each on a blue line separately. Three players are in the neutral zone playing against three players from the other team.

Procedure
To start the game, three players play against three players, all of whom are working to get possession of the puck for their team. After they get possession, they can pass the puck to the line and then move to get it back. Each successful pass is worth 1 point, but two players cannot pass it back and forth. Each pass must be to a different player in the game. The other team tries to disrupt possession of the puck so that they can work to make passes with their team. Shifts should last roughly 30 seconds. The coach blows the whistle to line change the group; players come in one side of their line and three new players go out the other.

Coaching Tips
- Players off the puck should be moving to get open by moving to open ice. For older players, the open ice can be anywhere because players can pass the puck to the line and then to the available player. Encourage players not to skate toward the puck because this can cause more of a problem. Players should try to find available ice to pass the puck to.
- Encourage players to pass the puck hard to their teammates whether they are in the game or on the side so that players get the puck quicker.
- Backhand passes and backhand receptions can happen in this game, so encourage players to make the plays as they come up. If they try to adjust their body to make what should be a backhand pass into a forehand pass, the passing lane may be different. The saying "Move the puck when you are supposed to, not when you have to" is applicable to this game.

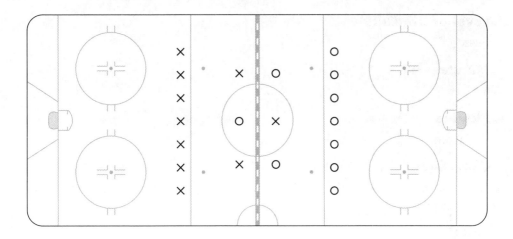

CROSS ICE 1 VS 1

Level of Difficulty

Easy

Minutes

6-8

Players

Full team

Objectives

To work on protecting the puck and advancing forward toward the other player's net.

Setup

Players play cross ice between two lines on the ice. Each player has a partner who acts as their goalie with their feet being the posts. One partner lines up to play 1 vs 1, and the other partner lines up as the waiting goalie as a rest before their next shift.

Procedure

To start the game, players have an NHL face-off in the middle of their game. Each player works to score on the opposing team's net. To score, the player must bring the puck inside the other circles and slide the puck on the ice between the goalie's feet. Players are not shooting the puck to score. Instead, they are sliding the puck after they have gained position on the defending player. After they score, they must go back to center and can then reattack the player with the puck. The shift lasts roughly 20 to 30 seconds. The goalies then come off the boards, and the player who was playing goes back to be the goalie. After both players have played against one team, the coach can slide one side of the boards down one zone, so that each team plays a new team in their second shift on the ice.

Coaching Tips

- This game starts to work on puck protection in a way that a turnover typically ends up in the net. Players should work to maintain possession of the puck and to go around opponents, not through them. As they get the hang of this game, players will find that they have the puck longer, even as the defender is trying to get the puck from them.

- The players with the puck should be working to look over their shoulder to see where pressure is and to find available ice.

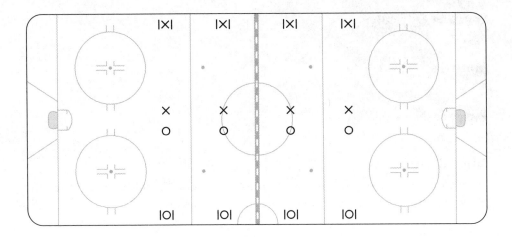

2 VS 1 BOX GAME

Level of Difficulty
Easy

Minutes
8-10

Players
Full team

Objectives
To have players work on moving the puck quickly and moving without the puck to create a passing option for the puck carrier.

Setup
Use four cones (or tires) to set up a box (size depends on the space you want to provide). Two offensive players are inside the box with one defensive player.

Procedure
On the whistle, the offensive players try to pass to each other as the defensive player tries to intercept the puck. If the defensive player intercepts a pass or deflects it outside the box, they get 1 point. If the offensive team can complete three passes in a row, they get 1 point. Shift length should be roughly 30 seconds, and players then switch to form new groups. Each player should play offense and defense.

Coaching Tips
- As a reminder, players should always have an idea of where the player without the puck is relative to where they are standing. The defensive players should have their head on a swivel and have an idea where the puck is going. Their stick position is hugely important in this game because they can influence where the puck goes and deflect pucks away before the pass can be completed.
- The offensive player can use deception with their eyes, hands, and feet to get the puck to the available player. They may also need to use a saucer pass to make the pass. The most important person in the game is the offensive player without the puck because they can give the puck carrier a passing option. Encourage players to move to get open.

Variation
- Players can be added to this game as they get better at it. Using more players forces the puck carrier to be more aware of where the available space is. Possible setups are 2 vs 2, 3 vs 2, and 3 vs 3.

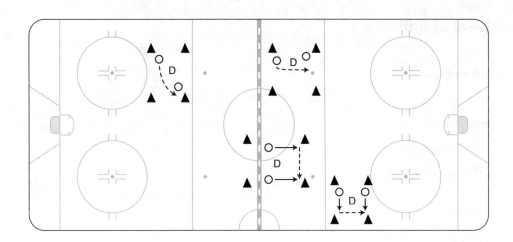

PUCK PROTECTION MAZE

Level of Difficulty
Easy

Minutes
6-8

Players
Full team

Objectives
To allow players to work on puck protection skills and communicating on the changes.

Setup
Set up two groups. Each player in the first group has a puck and works to protect it against a player in the second group, who does not have a puck. Players who do not have a puck try to disrupt the possession of the puck carrier in their time with that player. To start the game, each player is paired with someone else, one with a puck and one without a puck.

Procedure
On the whistle, the player with the puck works to protect it against the player without it. On the next whistle, the player with the puck must find another player to work against. Each group has their puck carrier leave and find another player to defend against. This rotation will happen one more time for a total of three small battles for each rep of the game. Players then switch possession of the puck and continue with the puck protection game. Each player should go three or four times before getting into the next part of practice.

Coaching Tips
- Remind players to use their body to keep the puck protected. Players often use just their hands to protect the puck and forget to use their bodies.
- Have the player who is protecting the puck think about puck location and work to keep it in a good spot.
- Encourage the defensive player to use their stick on the ice rather than across the offensive player's hips.

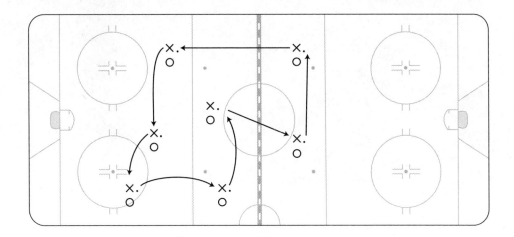

CHAPTER 4

Offensive and Defensive Games

Many games allow offensive concepts and defensive concepts to be developed, and coaches typically rely on these for their small-area games. These games can be the situations that start to connect what the coaches are teaching to what the players are able to execute in games. Games can revolve offensively around several scenarios:

- Scoring with 1 vs 0, 2 vs 0, 3 vs 0
- 1 vs 1 play with focus on puck protection
- 2 vs 1 play with focus on the player off the puck
- 2 vs 2 play with focus on supporting and protecting the puck
- 3 vs 2 play with focus on puck support and puck movement
- Timed games to put players under pressure to score
- Various areas of play with situations that come off the rush, off the wall, below the goal line, or net front

Defensive situations can be focused on the importance of defending first before going on the offensive side of the play:

- Starting each shift in the small-area game on defense before the offensive shift
- 1 vs 1 play with focus on taking away time and space
- 2 vs 1 play with awareness of taking away the most dangerous option
- 3 vs 2 play with focus on partner communication and spatial awareness
- 3 vs 3 with focus on player-to-player coverage or situations that build into defensive-zone coverage

Specific individual skills can be addressed for offensive concepts or defensive concepts. Depending on the game being used, coaches can add specific areas they would like to see from teaching progressions in practice that move one step closer to the game.

OFFENSIVE CONCEPTS AND SKILLS USED IN SMALL-AREA GAMES

I always build my practice plans around the idea that players need to build confidence in practice before it comes out in games. A focal point of planning is having each player work on concepts that will help them in practice to lead into small-area games and finish in matches. By focusing on specific skills, we as coaches should be able to see development of each player.

Skating Skills

The foundation on which the game is built is effective skating. Each player will be different in the development of their skating skills. When I work to develop offensive skating skills, I start with two areas. First, I look at skating speed and ways that we can develop more efficient strides through effective use of gliding, body position, stride length, stride location, stride recovery, stride rate, and upper-body control. After players have a basic understanding of good movement in a straight line, we add the second step, which involves puckhandling speed. Typically, when players get a puck, they slow down. My goal is to bring puckhandling speed up to skating speed without the puck. The goal is for players to go just as fast with the puck as they can without it. Additionally, players need to develop edge skills with one foot on the ice, which I call one-foot edge development (inside edge and outside edge working independently), two-foot edge development (turning, jam turns, punch turns, evasive maneuvers), linear crossovers to develop attack angles, and the ability to change direction through stops and starts.

Symmetry Skills

This idea involves developing players' puck skills on both their forehand and backhand so that as plays come up in the game, players can execute them without hesitation or adjustment. The goal is to have players develop the confidence to use both the forehand and backhand sides in various situations with puckhandling, puck protection, passing, pass reception, and shooting. Obviously, players will not shoot the puck with their backhand as hard as they can on their forehand, but they should have the confidence to puck protect, pass, or shoot on their backhand when that is the play to be made.

Areas where players typically have trouble is with backhand reception of passes or accuracy of backhand passes. Players who do not feel comfortable making short backhand passes typically adjust the puck back to their forehand. In practice they may be able to get away with it, but in games that passing lane may not be available. The goal is to help players make the play with either their forehand or their backhand.

Puck Possession

Players who have puckhandling skills are confident when they have a puck on their stick. In games, players will not have a puck on their stick for long, so they need to develop puckhandling skills in practice. Typically, you can identify players who are not comfortable with the puck because they will throw it away under pressure. Building advanced skills with puck possession can include topics such as skating through pucks on puck retrievals for defense or handling rims for forwards. Having an opportunity to use drills that revolve around puck possession under pressure will lead to more confidence and possession time on these types of plays in a game.

Vision

When I work with players on developing vision, I simply refer to it as scanning the ice with the intention of taking in information. For example, when players are entering the offensive zone on a zone entry, I try to have them scan the ice to identify three things:

1. Where are the defensive players?
2. Where is your support?
3. Where is the backchecking forward?

By quickly identifying these three things, players should gain an understanding of the options that are available to them to help create the best opportunity for a chance to the net. Through good skating posture, players can increase their ability to see the ice.

Players who have not developed the ability to scan the ice while they are skating typically miss options to move the puck to or are not able to identify options as they come up.

Players with good vision can handle the puck and scan the ice at the same time. This ability is valuable in many situations:

- In the defensive zone to help with breakouts
- In the neutral zone to help with regroups and passing
- In the offensive zone to help with puck possession

Good vision can be worked on with simple puckhandling drills in which players must turn their heads and look over their shoulders. Drills in which players must keep their eyes up and make decisions based on what they see will help them learn more about how this ability can help them in a game.

Puck Protection

Protecting the puck comes up a lot in games because whoever has the puck will have other players working to take it away. Sometimes, one player will be working against the player with the puck; other times, multiple players may be involved. For example, one player may be angling the player with the puck and steering them into more pressure. How players react under pressure depends on their confidence with the puck and their understanding of where their support options are. In situations down low in the offensive zone or on the wall, players may have to hang on to the puck and absorb contact or pressure. Players should instinctively think to move the puck away from pressure and put their body between the checking player and the puck. This movement of the puck and the use of the hips should reduce the checker's access to the puck. When players develop balance through their skating so that they are solid on their skates and can create open space through movement or move into open space, their confidence in their puck protection skills will go up quickly because opponents will not push them off the puck.

Passing and Pass Reception

Through practice leading up to the small-area games, players should be able to work on a variety of passes. Passing will change based on the distance of the pass, the passing angle, obstacles, and the puck location. Players must learn to react to what they see to advance the puck or create a chance and to receive the pass when it comes to them. As much as we want passes to be perfect, they will not be, and players need to be able to maintain possession of any pass and react as the puck comes to them. The general rule is that a puck within one stick length of the pass receiver is their responsibility. As players become more advanced, we can focus on topics like passing to shooters so that passers know where the pass needs to be to allow the pass receiver to shoot it quickly.

Shooting Skills

To develop good shooting skills, players have to learn to react to the situation and work to get a shot on goal. They need to learn to release the puck off either foot, to change the angle, and to take what is given to them based on what they see. A shot on goal is better than no shot on goal, and players can develop confidence in their shooting in a game-like situation to prepare them for games. Continue to encourage players to use their backhand as well if that is the shot that can come to the net. Players can continue to develop their shooting skills on their own by shooting at home.

Spatial Awareness

The concept of spatial awareness will help you establish which players can think through the game and move to open space or create open space by the way they move the puck (through either stickhandling or passing), by the way they move their feet, or by the way they react off other players. Their ability to create space can come from the angles they choose to attack defenders, their ability to create deception, or their ability to keep defenders away from the puck. They do this by protecting the puck or by using tactics such as offensive stick lifts or offensive stick taps to create additional space. Understanding space is also relevant when players are off the puck because they need to recognize the space where they can get the puck back.

Playing Without the Puck

Most of the actual game is played without the puck, so players need to learn how to get open to get the puck back. Working to open space or timing the play to be in the right lane at the right time is a skill that players need to be exposed to both in drills and in games. If done properly with good clips chosen for teaching moments, demonstrating this concept with videos can help players learn the value of playing without the puck. This idea should be addressed in practice and worked on through development of skating skills (timing) and puck movement skills.

Communication

At times players must call for the puck when they want it or are open. Players can also communicate by directing the puck carrier with something they see. Nonverbal communication can also help lead to offensive chances. Teammates who have chemistry can establish eye contact to help them understand exactly what each is going to do. Players should not be afraid to be vocal when they want the puck because calling can make a teammate's decision much easier. In practice sessions the coach should address communication as much as possible.

DEFENSIVE CONCEPTS AND SKILLS USED IN SMALL-AREA GAMES

Players need to learn the defensive side to the game to become effective players as they continue to advance in their hockey development. Players who learn to defend will earn additional ice time because those who can help keep pucks out of their own net have huge value. I try to work with players to ensure they understand the difference between checking and defending.

Checking

Proper checking involves moving forward toward an offensive player to take away time and space with good stick position, good skating (angle of attack), and good body position. No player likes to work with limited time and space. Teaching players in practice about checking is needed to help keep them safe. By teaching players about safety, you can help them understand when to check and when not to check. Teaching players to stay close to the wall under pressure and to absorb checks will help them manage the puck to protect it and get more comfortable playing under pressure. Teaching players good angling skills will help them be in a good position to steer someone where they want them to go and, when needed, to finish their check.

Defending

A player who is defending is simply moving backward and accepting the rush or play coming toward them. The defender's stick is in a good position, their skating helps control where the offensive player is going (the player must not get beat to a higher percentage spot) through good hip and shoulder position, and their body is always between the offensive player and the net.

Both checking and defending work when used at the right time in the game, but they do not work if they are used at the wrong time. Help players understand these concepts through practice and competitive situations so that they build confidence in their decision making when using them in an actual game.

Defensive Skating Skills

Players can work on skating in competitive situations from a defensive perspective with topics such as backward skating, stops and starts, transition skating, edge development, angles, and acceleration. By becoming good skaters when defending, players can quickly work to take away time and space and work to keep their body between the offensive player and the net.

Body Position

This topic can relate specifically to skating with a good spine angle to allow good vision and balance. Defensive players who are balanced and ready to engage physically make it harder for the offensive players to make plays or get close to the net. Body position can also relate to the position on the ice relative to the offensive player or puck. Keeping good defensive side positioning while being strong and engaged are crucial in the development of a player's defensive ability. Ideally, players are always between the offensive player and the net to ensure they do not get beat.

Stick Position

Brad McCrimmon, a former coach of mine, always said, "A good stick position will start your checking angle, take away time and space, and break up passes." (I have toned this down a little because he may have tossed a couple swear words in there when he said it!) When I pass on this advice to my players, they start to understand how useful their stick can be in either influencing the options of the puck carrier, putting pressure on the puck carrier, or breaking up a passing play.

Adding good stick situations into small-area games or encouraging good stick positions can help build players' confidence in their ability to break up plays with their stick. Small-area games always have situations where the coach can include having a good stick as an area of focus. This item may not be the focus for the game, but the coaches and players on the defensive side of the puck can always stress stick position as a key to breaking up plays.

Communication

As mentioned earlier, voice can be a powerful tool when used properly on the ice. Defensively, players can work on calling out what they see or communicating when they are off the puck to help make a teammate's decision making easier. This defensive skill is one that players can directly transfer into games and see some improvement.

I was once having trouble getting through to a team that absolutely would not communicate in practice. They would not talk to each other. They did not call for passes, call out what they saw, or help in decision making, no matter how many times I stopped what we were working on and asked them to talk. After this continued to happen, I decided to stop talking in practice myself to prove a point. The next time the team came to the board, I did not say a word. I drew up the drill but did not explain anything. I did not mention the key parts. All I did was quickly draw the drill one time. I stepped away from the board knowing what was about to happen, but I let the group work through it. I did not blow the whistle to start the drill, and I left it up to them to figure out what I drew (again to help prove my point). As I guessed, without me as their coach communicating what I wanted the drill to look like or what the key elements of the drill were, the players had no idea what to do. When we came back to the board and I explained the drill again (after sacrificing five minutes of practice to prove my point), the team came out talking like we had never heard before!

Shot Blocking

This important skill helps minimize the chances that get through to your net. Players must be willing to sacrifice their body to block shots. To practice this skill, I use games with sponge pucks to control the potential for injury.

When we teach shot blocking, we start at a young age to help players understand what the opposing team's shooting lane looks like and how to get their body in the way. As players become stronger and faster at recognizing shooting lanes, we encourage them to get a piece of the shot.

We teach players different ways to block shots and have them work to identify the situation in the game where they can use each one.

Here are some options we work through:

- On the feet with shin pads together when using forward momentum. If the player can move in the shooting lane toward the shooter, they should keep their shin pads together and take away space as well. The stick should be on the ice to take away a passing option.

- On one knee when forward progress is not possible. This happens a lot on penalty kills when the player wants to become as big and quick as possible to take away options to the net. This option can work well to deter a shooter from shooting and to help change the play to the net. This technique works best when the player is in the lane to the net and forces the shooter to move.

- When the player is out of the shooting lane and needs to get back into the shooting lane, they can slide. We do not stress this as the first option, but it can be effective when used in the right situation of the game. Players should time their slide to line up their shin pads with the shooting lane at the time the shooter is shooting the puck. As soon as they feel the puck hit them, the shot blocker can roll forward (in case the puck is under them) and then get up quickly to track the puck. Players should get back on their feet as quickly as possible after sliding.

Younger players often hesitate to get into shooting lanes because being hit by a puck hurts. Take time to work on this technique in practice and cheer when players block shots in small-area games. Players need to build up their courage to do this regularly in matches.

Spatial Awareness

Recognizing where ice is available and working to take it away is a key part of playing defense. Players need to recognize the puck carrier's options to move the puck and work to make sure that their stick is in the passing lane while blocking a lane to the net with their body. Players can work to shut things down with their feet and work to influence where they want the offensive player to go with the puck.

Defensive Vision

This idea revolves around play without the puck, recognizing how things are going to play out, and seeing the play develop. Being able to scan the ice to recognize passing options for the puck carrier and being able to take those options away is an example of good defensive vision. As the player turns to scan the ice, they also must recognize what the puck carrier is doing against them. Being able to manage what is happening both close to them and away from them requires a lot of practice.

Combining offensive and defensive concepts in the same game is great for your communication as a coach because you can easily work through the relevant areas with the players. Being able to identify specific things each day to have players focus on is key to their continued development. Challenging offensive players to play defense or defenders to play offense will help expand their skill sets and improve their understanding of what the other is trying to do come game time. Ultimately, the goal of using these types of games is to expose players to situations that will come up in matches.

CRASH THE NET

Level of Difficulty
Moderate

Minutes
10-12

Players
Full team—can go both ways from the red line

Objective
To promote rebounds, net-front plays, and pucks around the net.

Setup
Place nets back to back on the red line. Players are in the benches, and coaches stand behind the blue lines. If you have several coaches that is fine because for this game, the more coaches the better as long as they are divided equally. Coaches have pucks behind them in the event a puck is missed on a pass.

Procedure
On the whistle, three players come out of the box and work to get possession of the puck. After they gain possession, they can pass to their coaches (the coaches on the far blue line from their bench) and then work to get to the net (the net facing away from their bench). The coaches must quickly make a play toward the net to create a rebound, deflection, or puck scramble. If that team can score, the coaches throw a new puck into the game. If they do not score and the other team gains possession of the puck, they can pass to their coaches and work to get to the other net.

Coaching Tips
- With the nets being close, this game goes fast and changes quickly.
- Players should work on getting position around the net and keeping their sticks down around the net. They work to find loose pucks on scrambles and try to elevate pucks on rebounds.
- If players see that lanes are blocked for the coaches, they should work to become available in the direction of the net for a shot-pass deflection.

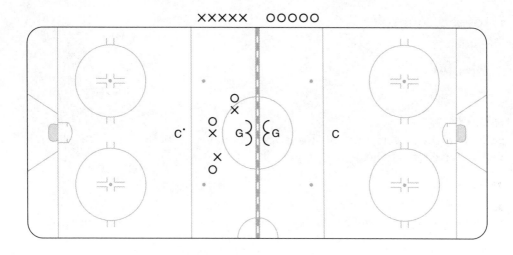

NET-FRONT BATTLE

Level of Difficulty
Moderate

Minutes
8-10

Players
Six to eight players and one goalie (can be played in both ends with a team if they have two goalies)

Objectives
To work in front of the net on rebounds or puck scrambles and to work defensively to clear the front of the net and get pucks out of the dangerous spots.

Setup
Place pucks just inside the top of the circle so that the coach can shoot pucks in on the goalie. The intent is to create a second puck battle in front. Split players into two even teams by jersey color. The game can start 2 vs 2 with one team designated on offense and one team designated on defense for the full shift, which can be three to five pucks depending on how long each puck goes. Players start on the hash marks with the defensive players on the hash mark closer to the net.

Procedure
The coach shoots a puck in on the goalie and tries to create a rebound. The players play that rebound wherever it goes in the zone. The offensive team tries to score, and the defensive team tries to break up possession and clear the puck. The goalie freezes all pucks around the crease. A whistle goes for the next puck to come in, but the players must touch "the nearest boards" before they can play the puck. This rule will create some separation in the players and different positions for the next battle. The coach can decide how many pucks come in for each shift. The teams change for the next shift, and the other team is on offense.

Coaching Tips
- At some point the players will realize that the "nearest boards" are behind the net and will come back to the net a little faster. Offensive players can look to tip or deflect pucks on the way through to create a tougher save for the goalie.
- Remind the defensive players to keep good body position on the defensive side of the battle (closer to the net) and work to control sticks in front to minimize the threat to score.

- As players get older, a physical element will come into this game as players learn to battle in front of the net. Winning these battles is a key part of games. Winning the battles in the offensive zone means getting chances to score. Winning the battles in the defensive zone limits offensive second-chance opportunities.

Variations

- This game can also be played 1 vs 1 to focus on specific movements and players.
- If you want your team to work on crashing the net, you could try 3 vs 3, which will create a lot of congestion in front, especially as players come back to the net after touching the boards.
- Another option is to have the player at the front of the line waiting at the top of the circle as a shooter on one side (offensive team) and an outlet on the other side (defensive line). This setup allows a pass from the net-front scramble so that the players engaged in the drill are aware of their surroundings.

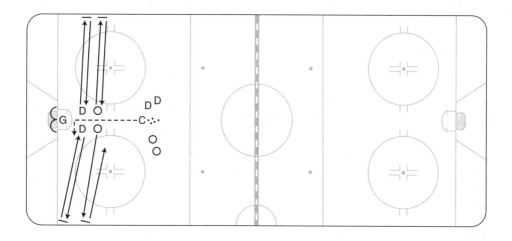

1 VS 1 HIGH AND LOW

Level of Difficulty
Easy

Minutes
8-10

Players
Four players to a full team (and at least one goalie)

Objectives
To work on high and low support in the offensive zone. On offense, to work on deciding which option for moving the puck is better as players move to the net; on defense, to work on keeping good defensive side positioning with the body between the offensive player and the net.

Setup
The offensive and defensive players start in the circle. One player is above the circle and one player is below the circle as passers. This setup can be a group of 4 in one end, a setup on each side of the zone with a group of 8 to 10, or a setup on both ends if you have your full team. The coach can have pucks in the middle of the ice to spot them in whichever corner the group starts in.

Procedure
The coach starts by throwing a puck into a space near the circle for the offensive player to get. The offensive player should have two options to move the puck to, one above them and one below them. The offensive player can use them if needed and then work to get open by the net. The goal is to have the player move the puck and jump to the net to work to create offense. If a passing lane is available, the offensive player should get the puck back. If no passing lane is available, the puck should be put on the net quickly. If a new puck is needed, the coach can spot a new puck into the game for the offensive player to get to. When the double whistle happens, the high and low players move into the circle and are the next two to go in the drill. A new player moves to fill the ice down below the offensive player.

Coaching Tips

- As a tight-area drill for defenders, they must work to keep good body position and good stick position, reacting to where the puck goes in the game. The idea of defensive side positioning is big in this game because defenders try to keep their bodies between the offensive player and the net.
- Offensively, the player should move the puck and move their feet to get into available space or move to the net to work to find a rebound. They can use the options above and below them rather than work through the defensive player. The offensive player should think about moving the puck and moving their feet.

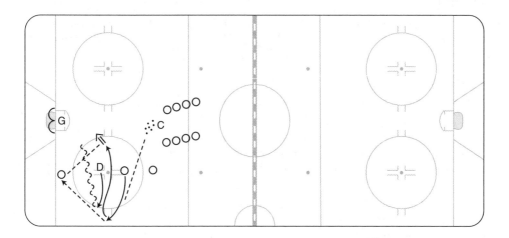

2 VS 2 BACKCHECK

Level of Difficulty
Hard

Minutes
8-10

Players
Full team

Objectives
To backcheck quickly to break up a play going to the net.

Setup
Teams set up on the blue line of each end. Two players from each group start in the zone to create two separate 2 vs 2 games, one in each end of the ice. The coaches have pucks in the middle of the blue line in each end.

Procedure
The coach throws a puck into the zone, and players play 2 vs 2 for a short time. Whichever team gets the puck is on offense, and the defending team works to get the puck back. The teams play to maintain possession on the first puck. One coach blows the whistle for both ends. The team that has the puck must have both players clear the top of the circle and then go to try to score. They have a quick 2 vs 0 before the other team arrives. The team that does not have the puck must backcheck to the other end and work to break up the play from the other group. If they can get back quickly enough, they continue to play 2 vs 2 for a short time.

Coaching Tips
- This drill is a hidden bag skate drill for the group because they must work to get back quickly to defend the other group. The group will start to anticipate the whistle, so encourage them to work to get that first puck back so that they don't have to backcheck to the other end. This will create another battle in the zone before the backcheck.

- One thing to note for this game is that colors of jerseys are not that important except for the first 2 vs 2 because once that one ends, the players could play against the same jersey color on the second 2 vs 2.

Variation
- This drill can also be 3 vs 3, but players will have to be aware in the neutral zone as they backcheck to the other side so that they do not run into each other.

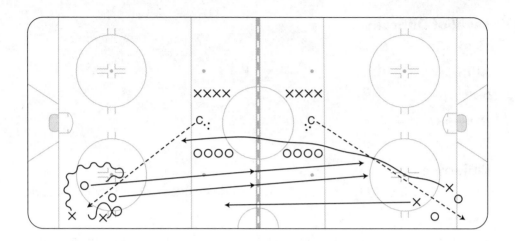

2 VS 2 IN ZONE

Level of Difficulty
Hard

Minutes
8-10

Players
Full team

Objectives
To work on gaining offensive position on the defensive team and trying to score.

Setup
Players are in groups of two lined up at the red line with pucks in their line. This game can be played both ways if you have enough players on each side (eight minimum). Two players start in the zone as defenders, and a player waits at the red line to start the game.

Procedure
The first offensive player starts the drill by passing to the D near the boards, who takes the pass and passes to the other defender. This defender moves and passes back to the first offensive player, who is moving on the boards to support the puck. This offensive player passes back to the next offensive player in line and goes around the dot, and these two offensive players attack the defenders on a 2 vs 2 rush. The defense must work to skate the puck over the top of the circle and then they are done. They go back to the line, and the offensive team becomes the next defenders. Rotation is offense to defense, defense rests. When this happens, the offensive team becomes the defensive team, and the next player starts the game again. The offensive team changes to the defensive team if the defensive team skates the puck out, if they score, if they shoot and the goalie freezes the puck, or if they shoot and the puck gets deflected out of play.

Coaching Tips
- In this puck possession game the defensive team plays a little bit tired after they have had an offensive shift. Encourage players to work on the defensive aspects of their game through good work with their feet and sticks.
- Offensively, encourage players to protect the puck and challenge players who are tired. Make them defend the net and work to get inside position on the defensive players. Whenever a player can get shoulder position on the defensive player, they should be driving the puck to the net. Players should work to create some form of a 2 vs 1 on the initial attack and attack with speed. Forwards will also be defending, so players may be working against someone who does not play defense regularly. Players should work

to create a situation where opponents feel uncomfortable. The goal here is to keep shifts short with the defensive team taking things away quickly.

Variations

- A second puck can be added in if the puck is cleared out by the defensive team without their skating the puck over the top of the circle. The puck can be spotted in or rimmed in to continue the play until the defensive team can skate the puck out.

- This game can be played both ways if you have enough players to make it work. This game gets harder because the offensive team controls the puck and the shift.

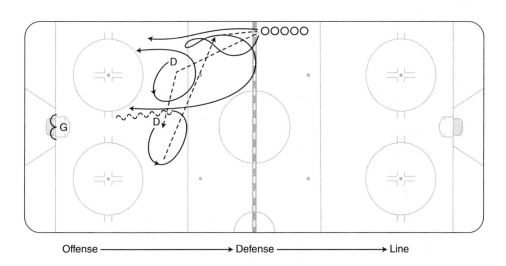

Offense ⎯⎯⎯⎯⎯⎯→ Defense ⎯⎯⎯⎯⎯⎯→ Line

SIDELINE GAME

Level of Difficulty

Easy

Minutes

8-10

Players

Full team

Objectives

To work on puck movement and supporting the puck.

Setup

The game is played cross ice. One team lines up on one side, and the other team lines up on the other side. The game is played 3 vs 3, and a coach controls the changes on a whistle.

Procedure

The game starts with a face-off and is played 3 vs 3. The team with the puck can pass the puck to their line and then work to get open to get it back. The idea of the game is to get the puck moving quickly and work to get available. The player on the outside who touches the puck must make a pass back into the middle of the ice where the game is and cannot pass the puck down the line. The players who are in the game should be looking to pass and move and get pucks to the other team's net as quickly as possible. When the whistle goes, three new players come in from one side of their line, and the three that are going out fill in the line at the other side.

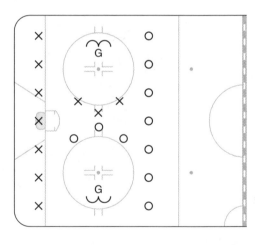

Coaching Tips

- This game works on improving communication and gets the whole group involved in the game.
- Puck movement is key, and players must be able to pass and move to become available to get the puck back.

3 VS 3 HIGH PLAYER IN OFFENSIVE ZONE

Level of Difficulty
Hard

Minutes
10-12

Players
Full team

Objectives
To work offensively on having a player above the puck in the offensive zone and to work defensively on the ability to outnumber players on the puck if necessary.

Setup
The game is played cross ice with 3 vs 3 on each side and the remaining players outside the blue line. The coach has pucks in the middle of the blue line.

Procedure
The game starts with a face-off and is played 3 vs 3. We set up an imaginary line through the middle of the ice surface that one of the offensive players must stay behind. The offensive team can rotate players in the zone (i.e., the same player does not have to stay high all shift). When the puck switches sides or changes possession, only two of the offensive players can go deeper into their offensive zone. A coach blows the whistle for line changes and spots a new puck if needed.

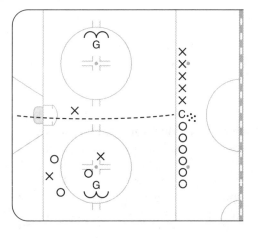

Coaching Tip
- This game requires a high level of awareness about where the puck is and where the other players are. The coaches will see the players who can support the puck even when they are the high player in the zone and those who can rotate out of the high spot as another player comes out.

NEUTRAL-ZONE PROTECT YOUR NET

Level of Difficulty
Moderate

Minutes
8-10

Players
8-10

Objectives
On defense, to enforce defensive side positioning and have an active stick; on offense, a puck protection game to work against a defensive player and work to get into available ice.

Setup
The game is useful as a third station in the neutral zone, or it can be played in all circles. Place two cones (or tires) on the edge of the neutral-zone circle on each side. Two players are in the circle to create a 1 vs 1 in the circle. One puck is added in, and the offensive player (with the puck) tries to skate the puck through the other player's net (i.e., between the cones). The defensive player works to keep their body position between their net and the offensive player while trying to gain possession of the puck.

Procedure
After the game starts, the offensive player works to get the puck through the net by skating it for a point, and the defensive player tries to keep the offensive player away from the net and keep their body between the net and the offensive player. The defensive player works to cause a turnover and take away time and space. If the puck leaves the circle, a new puck is added in and the game continues. All extra pucks should be placed outside the circle because this game goes through a lot of pucks. Shifts can last roughly 30 to 45 seconds, and then a new 1 vs 1 starts.

Coaching Tip
- Encourage players to engage physically by taking away time and space quickly so that the puck carrier does not have space to work in. By pushing the offensive player away from the net, the defensive player can create space to recover into should they need it.

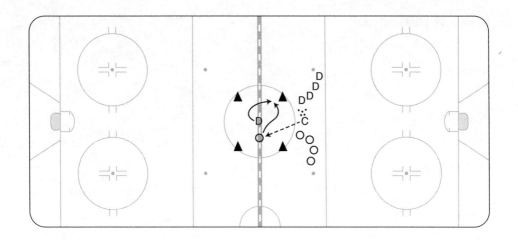

3 VS 2 CLEAR THE LINE

Level of Difficulty
Moderate

Minutes
8-10

Players
Full team

Objectives
To work on supporting the puck and offensive attack options.

Setup
Three offensive players line up at the blue line ready to attack against two defenders.

Procedure
This game is played with movement to the net on the first two pucks, and the third puck can be played out in the corner. The defensive players work to break up the puck through pressure and positioning. The offensive players must get back onside before the coach spots the second and third pucks. The coach spots a puck for the three offensive players to try to score. When that initial rush is finished, the coach blows the whistle. The three offensive players must get back onside outside the blue line and reattack against the defensive players. After the second rush, the coach blows the whistle and the offensive players must get back onside to attack a third time. The defenders must work to take away space and adjust to where the offensive players are. The third rush can play out in the corner if the play allows it.

Coaching Tips
- This game is useful to play after a day of working on offensive attack options or rush specifics. The game allows offensive rushes to happen, and you will be able to see who is able to make reads in the game setting when things are not perfect. Each regroup will put players in different spots, and some players will not want to drive the net if they are the closest player to the puck.
- Watch for the details and have one coach working to talk to the group when they come off their shift.

Variation

- If the group is doing well 3 vs 2, a backchecker can be added to make this 3 vs 3. The backchecker starts at the red line and hurries back for the initial rush. When the whistle goes, the backchecker must touch the red line and stop before coming back into the zone.

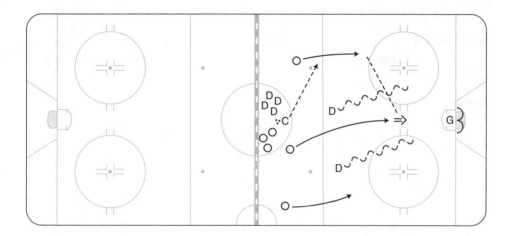

2 VS 2 HALF ICE—PLAYERS WAITING

Level of Difficulty
Hard

Minutes
8-10

Players
Full team

Objectives
To work on taking away time and space defensively before going on offense with the puck.

Setup
Nets are placed across the ice from each other, and the group is divided into two teams. The teams are split up and lined up across the blue line. The coach has the pucks in the middle of the ice to spot a new puck into the game if needed.

Procedure
The game starts 2 vs 2 and is played in half the zone. An imaginary line runs through the zone where two new defensive players are waiting close to the line in their end. When the defensive team gains possession of the puck, they are then on offense and can attack against the two waiting players. After the two offensive players leave their defensive zone to try to score, two new players fill in behind them and wait defensively. When the defending team gets possession, they attack against the two new players who are waiting for them. The game goes back and forth with two new players jumping in each time the puck leaves the zone. The rotation (after the first shift) is start on defense, go on offense, go to the back of the line.

Coaching Tips
- This game can be quick, so lots of communication is required among the players. They must be ready to jump in and play in the event that a sudden turnover occurs.
- This game is about maintaining puck possession to score.

Variation

- This drill can be used as a net-front game as well by having the two new defensive players be active on the rush and allowing them to shoot if they get a puck passed to them. Normally, this game is not played with the two new players shooting because it is designed to be a puck possession game with defensive side positioning, but this option can be added if your team needs work on net-front play. As soon as the defensive team gets possession of the puck, they attack the two waiting players.

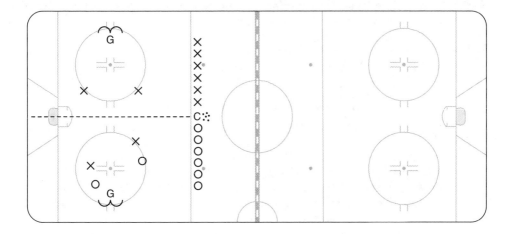

3 VS 2 FORECHECK

Level of Difficulty

Hard

Minutes

10-12

Players

Full team

Objectives

To work on getting to pucks first and getting angles to help steer the puck in the desired direction.

Setup

Three offensive players and two defensive players line up on the blue line ready to go. The coach dumps the puck into the corner, where the defensive players try to get to it and the offensive players try to get it back.

Procedure

The game starts when the coach dumps the puck into the corner. The two defensive players must recognize how the offensive team is forechecking, and the player off the puck must work to become available. The offensive team must work to get the first player on the puck with a good angle to steer the puck into the next player. As soon as they get the puck stopped, the second player can join the battle and work to get the puck. The third player can slide over and be on the puck side in a high position in the slot, available for a pass. The shift can continue for a time designated by the coach. A new puck is added when the goalie freezes the puck, the puck is in the back of the net, or the defense skates the puck out of the zone.

Coaching Tip

- This game offers a good opportunity to see how players forecheck, who is willing to get to the puck first, and who is willing to protect the puck under pressure. It will also make clear what the players need to work on in practice.

Variations

- The game can be changed to have the players starting at different levels, which will give the defensive team a better chance to get to the puck first, putting the offensive team into a forechecking scenario. If the players all start at the blue line (or top of the circle), the offensive team will get to the puck in some situations.
- This game can also be played 3 vs 3 with three offensive players and three defensive players to simulate a game.

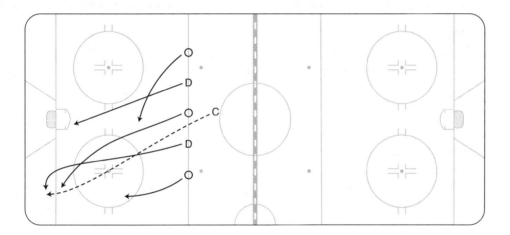

1 VS 1, 2 VS 2, 3 VS 3

Level of Difficulty
Easy

Minutes
8-10

Players
Full team (can be split into both ends)

Objective
To work on defensive vision off the puck as well as defensive position.

Setup
Six players set up in the zone, three on offense and three on defense. The players set up in pairs with two in each corner and two in the high slot.

Procedure
On the whistle, the coach spots a puck to the first 1 vs 1 in one of the corners. They play a short 1 vs 1; the offensive player tries to score, and the defensive player defends. On the next whistle, the coach spots a puck to the second corner where the first two players join them to play 2 vs 2. On the third whistle, the coach spots a puck to an available corner. The third pairing goes to get it, and the other four players join in to make it 3 vs 3.

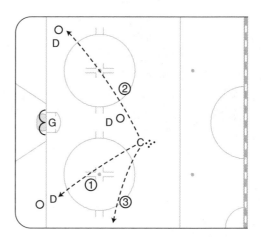

Coaching Tips
- Remind players that good defensive position and sticks are necessary to keep pucks away from the net.
- Players should always be able to see the player they are checking and the puck.
- Defensive players must work to take away time and space and force the offensive players to make quicker decisions.

Variation
- This game can be played in the end zone or, if needed, in the neutral zone with a 1 vs 1 on each side of the net and a third 1 vs 1 in the slot.

ADD A PLAYER

Level of Difficulty
Moderate

Minutes
10-12

Players
Full team

Objectives
Work to get a game of 2 vs 2 going and add players to make it up to a 4 vs 4 shift. The concept of the game is to recognize that a power-play opportunity could develop if you add players to your team to make it harder to defend against.

Setup
Players play cross ice 2 vs 2, and the rest of the players wait in a line at the blue line. The coach is in the middle of the teams in a position to spot the puck or add a new puck if the puck leaves the zone.

Procedure
Each shift starts as a 2 vs 2. During that shift, if a team passes back to the line and then receives a return pass, the first player in the line can jump into the game to make it a 3 vs 2. This can happen again to make it four players on one side playing against two, three, or four players on the other team.

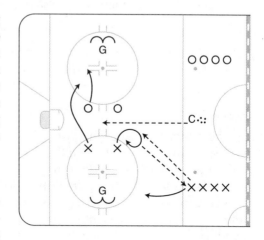

Coaching Tips
- Encourage players to recognize situations that will produce good offensive chances toward the net.
- Players should move the puck quickly and work to get open when they do not have the puck so that the puck carrier has passing options.
- Defensively, players need to identify situations and have an active stick to make themselves look bigger and take away passing lanes. When a player gets a chance to pass to their line, they should do it to add a player to their group.
- Keep shifts short and keep the energy of the group high. This game is always changing, and the situations in a shift can change quickly, much like in a game.

SLOT BOX GAME

Level of Difficulty
Easy

Minutes
8-10

Players
Full team

Objective
To work in a confined area to get pucks back to the net quickly.

Setup
Create a box by placing two tires (or cones) on the back wall in line with the dots and two tires (or cones) at the top of the circle. The coaches pass pucks in from outside the box on the sides. Divide the players into two teams, who wait outside the box. The game starts with three offensive players in the box and two defensive players (plus a goalie to make 3 vs 3). The coaches pass in five to seven pucks, alternating sides on each puck to ensure that players move. A new puck comes in when one of three things happens:

1. The puck ends up in the back of the net from a goal.
2. The puck is frozen by the goalie.
3. The puck is cleared outside one of the three sides of the box. The fourth side is the back boards, and that side is in play.

Procedure
On the whistle, the coach spots a puck to the offensive team, and they make a play, trying to score. When one of the three things described in the setup section happens, a new puck from the other coach is spotted in and the offensive players try to score. The defensive team tries to pressure the offensive team and create a loose puck so that they can deflect it away from the net and get it outside the box. When the puck goes outside the box, a new puck gets spotted into the game. This action continues until the coaches run out of their five to seven pucks. Players then change.

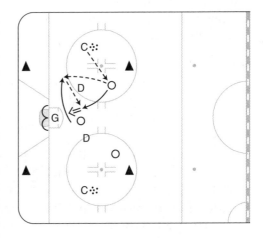

Coaching Tips

- At some point in the game, the offensive team will skate the puck outside of the box as they work to find available ice. You should stop them and throw a new puck into the game so that they learn that the game has a boundary.
- Many younger players like to skate away from pressure instead of standing and protecting the puck from the defender.
- This game is most effective when players move to get open and get shots toward the net.
- The plays do not have to be high-level passes with backdoor tap-ins. Instead, players must simply work to get pucks on the net and create shots and rebounds. With only one net being used, this game can be played in both ends.

Variations

Many variations to this game can be used:

- 2 vs 2 game in the boxed area.
- 2 vs 1 game in the boxed area.
- 3 vs 2 with pass from below the goal line—for this game the coach always spots a new puck below the goal line, and the offensive team works on making passes out from below the goal line to the slot. After play on that puck ends (either in the net, covered, or cleared outside the box), a new puck is added and a new offensive player rotates down below the goal line to be the passer. Three pucks are used per shift (one per offensive player) before a new team is rotated in on offense.
- 3 vs 2 with designated passer—this game has a 2 vs 2 in front of the net with an offensive player below the goal line as a passer. This game is effective when following a day of rims or offensive-zone play because a coach can rim a puck into the passer, which forces the player to handle the puck and look to make a play by moving into available ice below the goal line. The coach can choose the number of pucks they want the players to handle and keep the shifts short to keep the game moving. The player below the goal line must work on getting clean possession on every puck that comes around the wall to them and making a pass to the offensive players who are in front of the net. If the puck carrier decides that no passing option is available and they have a lane, they can walk out and try to make a play toward the goalie as they would in a game. They must remember that they will be the player who releases below the goal line to get the net rim after that puck is finished. After the shift ends, the coaches can rotate the team on offense and designate a new passer. This game works best when everyone takes a turn at the passing role.

NEUTRAL-ZONE TWO-PUCK GAME

Level of Difficulty
Moderate

Minutes
10-12

Players
Full team

Objectives
Read and react to pucks in the neutral zone to be on either offense or defense.

Setup
Place nets up at the blue line facing each other. Teams line up on opposite sides of the line. This game is tough on the goalies because they are facing 2 vs 0 repeatedly or 1 vs 0 with the other goalie facing a 2 vs 1. Pucks are with the players on opposite sides of the blue line.

Procedure
On the whistle, two players from each team move into the middle to try to score. Both players must touch the puck before they can score. The game gets hard here. One player can defend the net and force the other team into a 2 vs 1 and leave the teammate going in on a 1 vs 0. But if they miss the net or the teammate scores, the player must be able to release to get in on the offense when they can. Both players must touch the second puck as well before they can score. Each shift is a race between the two teams to score two goals. Two goals in this game earns 1 point for the team.

Coaching Tips
- I tell the players the rules to this game, but I leave out that they can defend the other team. I let them figure out that they can.
- They also need to figure out when they can leave the defending position and become available to play offensively.
- In this game I ask the goalies not to shoot the puck down the ice; the players will do that themselves as they try to score.
- This game promotes player communication, and coaches can see the players working together.

Variation
- This game can be played 3 vs 3 as well with the same rules if you are playing with a full team or a bigger group and two goalies.

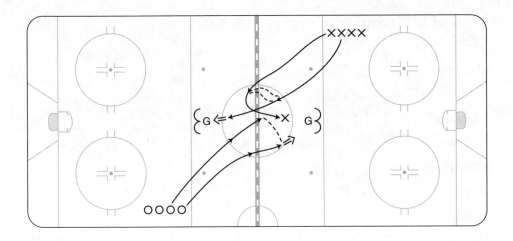

1 VS 1 CONFINED SPACE

Level of Difficulty
Easy

Minutes
8-10

Players
Full team

Objective
To work in a confined space where players must play 1 vs 1.

Setup
Place both nets roughly a face-off circle apart in a certain area of the ice. Players line up on both sides of the coach, who has pucks off to the side of the nets. One player from each group starts in the middle of the zone and gets ready to play 1 vs 1.

Procedure
The coach spots a puck into the zone, and the game is on. Each player works to score goals. When they do not have the puck, they must defend against the attacking player. Shifts are short in this game to keep everyone engaged. New pucks are added anytime the puck leaves the confined area or anytime a new group starts.

Coaching Tips
- Defensive players' sticks are hugely important in this setup. Encourage defenders to work to take away shooting lanes and deflect pucks away from the attacking player.
- Challenge offensive players to get into scoring areas more often, get shots on the net, and look for rebounds.

Variation
- This game can be played with less space and more players, making the game a 2 vs 2 or 3 vs 3.

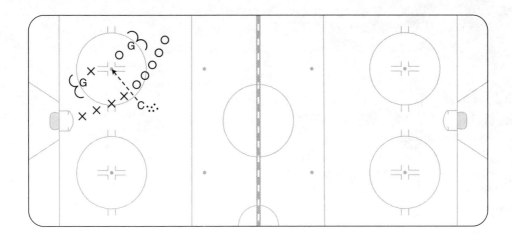

CHAPTER 5

Specialty Team Games

As the games become more competitive, situations with power plays and penalty kills become more important in winning hockey games. Allowing players to work in competitive situations more in practice will prepare them for situations that come up in the games. Paul Maurice, head coach of the Florida Panthers, once said, "If our penalty kill stops their power-play chance, that is one less goal we have to score to win the game." As a coach, you want to expose players to the power-play environment where their offensive skill sets must come out and penalty-kill situations where they must rely more on their defensive skill sets.

The Montreal Canadiens' 2021 playoff run showed how effective a good penalty kill can be when they went 13 games without allowing a goal on their penalty kill, spanning more than 30 power plays for the opposing teams. Their penalty kill was effective because they were fast and tenacious, worked together, and communicated through each shift on the ice. After seeing them play the way they did in the playoffs that season, other teams surely recognized how effective a team can be on the PK when players buy into what they are doing.

POWER-PLAY OPPORTUNITIES

Specialty team games play an important role in developing team success in higher-level hockey players. Here are some of the areas that are enhanced by playing specialty games.

Passing Options

Players can learn to support the player with the puck by giving them multiple passing options. If only one option is available, the defending team will know exactly where the puck is going. By having options, the puck carrier becomes more of a threat and can make the best decision possible. Players quickly realize that the players without the puck are often more important than the player with the puck. Furthermore, they learn that pressure from the penalty-killing team can stop one player but that they will have difficulty stopping a team who moves to support the puck and passes the puck well.

Team Systems

Team systems can be built into a game to help illustrate what the coach wants to see. A game could be a setup off the half wall or with the puck at the top with passing options on the flanks. If the coach's game plan revolves around shots coming to the net, the small-area game could focus on rebounds and net-front battles. Adding these elements into small-area games gives players more opportunities to work on the desired result.

Decision Making

Time and space can be reduced to force players to make quicker decisions. When the actual zone becomes available to them, making decisions should become easier because the players will have more time to move the puck and more space to move their feet.

Skill Transfer

Individual skill sets are directly transferable from practice into games. Puck skills like composure and confidence can be built up through practice and then executed in small-area games. These games will help high-level coaches get a good idea of which players can execute power-play situations and which players need to continue to develop those skills. Having a player on defense who can get the puck through traffic from the blue line is extremely useful on the power play. Players who constantly get shots blocked in practice in small-area games will not suddenly get shots through in games. Those players may have to spend some time working to get their heads up so that they can create and then use available shooting lanes.

Player Support

A good power play revolves around puck movement and player support. Encourage players to pass the puck hard and send it to a good spot in practice. A good spot means that the player who is receiving the pass can do something with the puck when it hits their stick. If a player is passing to a teammate who is in a shooting position, the passer should work to put the pass in a spot where the shooter can shoot. Good passing and receiving skills are hugely important for a good breakout to get up the ice and into the offensive zone, as well for the offensive-zone setup to create offensive chances.

Offensive and Defensive Zones

As much as we want the small-area games to focus on specific areas in the offensive zone, games can be played as well to work on breakout and puck retrievals to escape pressure in the defensive zone. If one player is pressuring down the ice, the multiple players who are coming back should be able to pass the puck to beat that one player's pressure. The ability to read pressure and move to available ice is a skill that requires a quick reaction to what is happening in the game. Your team can work on and practice this skill.

PENALTY-KILL OPPORTUNITIES

Adding small-area games to practice allows players to focus on specific areas that directly transfer into killing penalties in games. By adding specific games, the coaches can watch players and identify areas they need to improve on before putting players in those game situations.

Footwork and Skating

Players can learn to take away time and space quickly by the combination of footwork and stick position. Correct technique will put the offensive players in a more difficult spot because they will have to make decisions faster and the defensive player will be influencing the decisions they will be making. Good balance and good skating are crucial. Encourage players to work on edges and skating to close off lanes quickly. When they get a chance either to jump to a free puck or to jump a player to put pressure on them, they can do it quickly and with balance.

Stick Position

Players can learn to use their sticks effectively with one hand to steer opponents, to take away space by appearing bigger, and to block passing lanes while also recognizing when they need to use two hands to battle and tie up sticks around the net or in the corner. Players are often caught with their stick in the wrong lane or in the air, allowing skilled offensive players to pass pucks through the available lanes. Players will be surprised how often their stick can break up a play simply by being in the correct lane. Creating loose pucks or disrupting possession in games means that your team gets an opportunity to get possession, clear the zone, and potentially line change.

Using Spatial Awareness Effectively

Players who have developed spatial awareness can recognize dangerous threats in the speed and pressure of a game situation. Players must continually scan the ice and take in information. Learning to know who is on the ice against them and what hand those players shoot with is an important mental note that each player can make to help reduce the danger of the opponents' chances that come to the net when they are down a player. Coaches at all levels can know what the other team is trying to do in the power play by either viewing a video of a previous game or watching the first power play from the opposing team. After you have an idea what the other team is working to do, you should be doing something to shut down that option and force the opposing team to do something they are not as comfortable with.

Blocking Shots

Shot blocking, or denying pucks to the net, reduces the danger of the opponents' scoring opportunities. The goalies and players must be on the same page so that everyone understands what happens with shots on goal. Players often work to block shots, which is great and is a valuable component to effective penalty killing, but another element to consider is what is going to happen if the player does not block the shot. If the offensive player does a good job and gets the puck past the shot blocker, the goalie should have an idea of the available options based on what the shot blocker took away. Here, players need to be on the same page to deny prime scoring chances or increase the goalie's chance to make the save. Take, for example, a shooter shooting from the flank on the power play. If the shot blocker does their job, they will block the shot. If they fail to do their job and the opponent shoots it past them, there should be little chance that the puck can go to the far side of the net. The available lane to the net should be on the short side where the goalie can prepare and make that save. If the shot beats the goalie over the far shoulder, the shot blocker probably was not in the correct lane.

Communication

Communication is a big part of the defensive aspect of the game. Small-area games can help players learn to communicate and work together. Players should learn to communicate loudly and clearly so that teammates can easily understand them. By communicating to a teammate, a player helps them decide what they are going to do before they have to think about it. A player can be a teammate's eyes if they are under pressure and help them make their next play a positive one. For example, consider a player under pressure who is racing to a loose puck. On their way there, the player hears a teammate yell, "Chip." When the player gets to the puck, they will probably chip it because the teammate helped them make that decision. Likewise, goalies should be encouraged to communicate what they see to the defensive players.

Communication from the coach in small-area games can help players see success in games. In practice, players can talk to the coaches after each repetition of the drill. Coaches have an excellent opportunity to give players positive feedback or correct anything that needs improvement. During this time in practice, coaches will also be able to watch their team's play improve after they have provided some things to work on.

SHIFT SIMULATION

Small-area games that revolve around specialty teams are most effective when they are used to simulate a shift. That occurs when offensive players and defensive players do not shift from offense to defense in the middle of the shift or game. Multiple games in the zone with small areas using an odd number of players can also be effective (e.g., 3 vs 2 on each half of the zone) because players from the penalty kill can move the puck to their power play and vice versa for the other team. This setup allows groups of players to work together to help others succeed. This would be the situation where the penalty-killing side gets the puck to the power-play side to create chances. Having designated players in each role also allows the goalie to scan for dangerous players without constantly worrying about who is on offense in a quick-transitioning game. Players can work together to keep their end (or area) clean defensively for the length of their shift. Offensive players can also learn the importance of puck possession and making plays not only to create chances but also to capitalize on chances.

This time in practice is a good time to have everyone on your team work through the power-play scenarios and rotate through the penalty-kill scenarios. You as the coach can watch everyone and evaluate where they are good and where they need work. Players get lots of reps of drills that simulate those situations in games. The more reps that a player can get at each specific area, the more success they will have in games when they must make a decision under pressure.

END-ZONE POWER PLAY

Level of Difficulty
Moderate

Minutes
10-12

Players
Full team

Objectives
To work on simple puck support and puck movement in the end zone where players have an advantage.

Setup
Divide players to form two teams, and place the nets on the goal line at the bottom of the circle. You can place tires or cones between the hash marks to divide the zone in half, or players can just imagine a line there that only the puck can cross. Start with three offensive players and two defensive players in each space. The three offensive players on one side work with the two defensive players on the other side.

Procedure
When the puck is dumped into the zone, the group with two players tries to get the puck to their power-play side. The power-play side tries to score on the goalie. The play goes from side to side, and each group gets a short time on the power play because they will be under pressure and things will happen fast. Each shift should last one minute to give players an idea of what a shift feels like in the game. Rotate players on the whistle and make sure that players are killing penalties and working on the power play.

Coaching Tips
- Encourage the penalty-killing team to work on clearing the puck to the other side so that their power play can start with the puck. If they rim the puck to the other side, the offensive players will have to handle the puck off the wall. Encourage players to anticipate what is happening and help support the puck so that the power-play players are not chasing the puck to start their time on the power play. Constant chasing of the puck will minimize the offensive chances.
- Work with the penalty killers on stick position to take away time and space and deny passing lanes. If an offensive player wants to get the puck past a defensive player, they must either use a saucer pass or adjust their hands to make the play.

- This game is useful after you have spent time working on rims because you can throw a new puck in around the boards and pucks often switch sides on the wall. Players must prepare for the puck with their feet and their stick and read pressure and support.

Variation

- If your group is a little smaller you can play this game as a 2 vs 1, but it is more difficult for the single defending player.

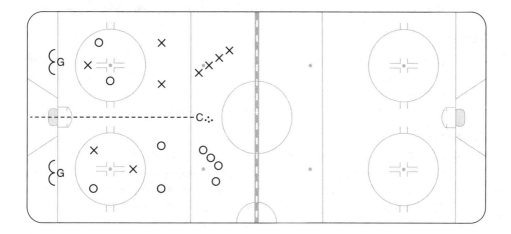

NETS BACK TO BACK POWER PLAY

Level of Difficulty
Moderate

Minutes
10-12

Players
Full team

Objectives
To establish spacing between players and puck support through movement.

Setup
Divide players into two teams. Place the nets back to back between the hash marks to cut the zone in half. The coach has pucks in the middle of the blue line to spot new pucks into the game when needed. On each side of the zone, start with three offensive players and two defensive players.

Procedure
On the whistle a puck is dumped into the zone to allow one side to play on a power play (3 vs 2) in a tight space. They should move the puck and move their feet to get open for the puck carrier. The other side waits for either a puck that misses the net, a puck that is frozen by the goalie, or a goal. If one of those three things happens, their side gets to go on offense to try to score. Shift lengths, controlled by the coach, should allow players to have an offensive chance and allow the other side to defend.

Coaching Tips
- This game promotes quick shots based on the distance from the net and has net-front play that includes scrambles and rebounds. If your team needs work in those areas, this is a great game.
- Encourage the defensive team to take away the most dangerous option to the net and force the offensive team to score in a different way. Players should have that mindset when they get into games. Encourage the defensive team to take away passing options and force the offensive team to make good plays to score. The defensive team should constantly be working to take away time and space.
- One thing to note in this game is to make sure that players are aware of where the puck is so that they do not get hit with the puck when they are not looking. This idea pertains particularly to the waiting goalie.

Variation

- A harder variation of this game is to have one of the penalty killers from the other side be down in the area beside the net to be a low passing option for the power play. The player would be located in the space between the nets. The player cannot score, but they create another option for the defenders to worry about. This option should be added only when teams have played this game 3 vs 2.

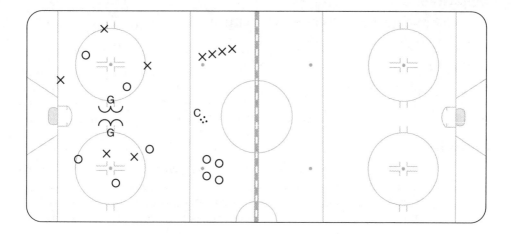

2 VS 2 LOW-TO-HIGH POWER PLAY

Level of Difficulty
Moderate to hard

Minutes
10-12

Players
Full team

Objectives
To get the puck to the point and encourage point shots toward the net to create offensive chances.

Setup
Divide the players into groups of two. Players with the same-colored jerseys are teammates. Teams rotate from shooting from the point to playing offense to playing defense (so that they are a little tired when playing defense).

Procedure
With a 2 vs 2 starting in the zone, the coach spots a puck to the offensive players. As quickly as they can, they pass the puck to the point and get to the net. The players who are playing the point must shoot or pass toward the net as quickly as they can. If no players are at the net, they can work to jump on the rebound or work to move to the net quicker when they see the puck there. The players who are converging to the net must work to get open and to avoid having their stick tied up when a loose puck is sitting there. The coach controls the shift length to allow several pucks to be thrown in so that players can work on getting pucks from low to high and then work to get to the net. Anytime the players at the blue line touch the puck, they should be making a play to the net with either a pass or a quick shot. One team shoots for the other team so that when they rotate into the game, they are against a team with different-colored jerseys.

Coaching Tips
- This game is effective for net-front play and point shots with a purpose. Players need to be able to get shots from the blue line to the net for this game to be effective. Encourage players to work to get to the net to jump on loose-puck rebounds or work to get available in a space close to the net where the puck is coming.
- Encourage the defending players to tie up sticks and clear lanes to the puck so that the goalie can see the puck.
- The offensive players will be working to take away sight lines to the net, so defending players want to work to keep those lines to the puck clear.

Variation

- This game can be played as a 3 vs 2 game as well with pucks coming to the net quickly anytime a point player touches the puck to allow high tips and players rolling with pucks to keep their eyes on the puck. The third player also opens up the option in the slot off the half wall or from down low. Their reaction to a puck that goes to the top must be quick because it will happen quickly in a game. Adding in the third player messes up the rotation a bit, but it creates a good option and requires the defenders to react to deny a dangerous option and clear rebounds. The third player offensively should be added only to a team (or group) that can move the puck well and get shots through because the shooter must work on shooting with their eyes up to see the available lanes.

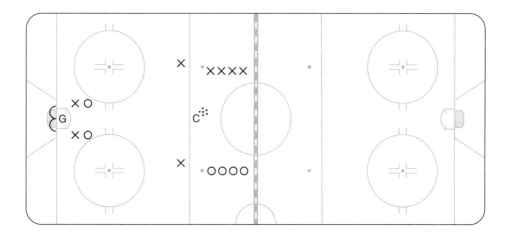

5 VS 4 TIMED SHIFT

Level of Difficulty
Moderate

Minutes
10-12

Players
Full team

Objectives
To work within a time frame trying to score.

Setup
Set up a penalty-killing team (four players on) and a power-play team (five players on). The coach can have spare pucks at the blue line.

Procedure
The coach designates the length of each power play (30 seconds, 45 seconds, 60 seconds). Each play starts with a face-off. The team on the power play works to score, and the team on the penalty kill works to kill that time down to zero. The power-play team should work to get the puck to the net quickly and move it around to create good offensive chances. The power-play players should work to move in the structure of your team and run options based on what they have worked on previously.

Coaching Tips
- This game is a good way to work on things with the pressure of the clock on the minds of the players. The additional pressure forces players to move to space that is not available or to do things that are not constructive for your team.
- Encourage players to continue to work within their structure and move the puck to the available players quickly. Support and quick puck movement are what will create good offensive chances to the net.
- This game is useful for re-creating end-of-game scenarios with 45 seconds, 30 seconds, 15 seconds, or 10 seconds to try to get something to the net or keep it away from the net.

Variation
- This game also works 5 vs 3 with a shortened clock to try to score quickly on the power play.

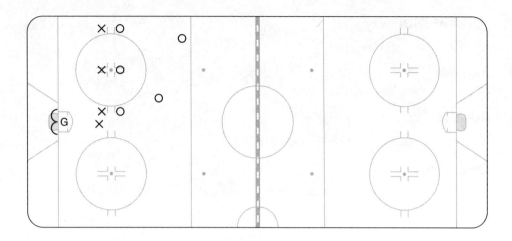

POWER-PLAY PUCK RETRIEVAL

Level of Difficulty

Hard

Minutes

6-10

Players

Six to eight players with no goalies needed

Objectives

To work on retrieving the puck under pressure from the penalty-killing team.

Setup

Divide players into two teams. Three players from one team and one player from the other start. The team with three players has players at the blue line, and the pressuring player is in the middle circle.

Procedure

When the coach dumps the puck into the zone, the retrieval team must go back and get it and move the puck away from the pressuring forward. The three players who are breaking out the puck should work to come out of the zone together (in your team's power-play breakout) after they have moved the puck away from the pressure of the opposing player. If they can skate the puck back over the blue line with control, they get 1 point. If the pressuring forward causes a missed pass (drastically missed) or maintains possession of the puck, they get 1 point. Switch teams for the next shift so that each group gets to break out a puck while the other team pressures.

Coaching Tip

- This game is useful for a day when you have one goalie (or a day when the goalie coach needs extra time with the goalies), and you can use one end without any shooting. Players can focus on puck support and moving to an area so that the puck carrier can easily move the puck away from the pressure of the one penalty killer. After the pressure is beaten, the puck can be moved back to a spot where it can be broken out smoothly.

Variation

- This game can move into a full puck retrieval drill when the group realizes how hard they have to work to get the puck away from pressure to open ice. This can lead into a full power-play and penalty-killing scenario in practice.

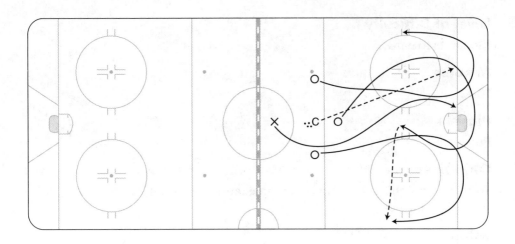

3 VS 4 SHOT BLOCKING

Level of Difficulty
Moderate to hard

Minutes
10-12

Players
Full team

Objectives
To focus on getting into shooting lanes and preventing shots from getting through to the net.

Setup
Have two offensive players at the blue line and one offensive player at the net playing against four penalty killers. The coach spots sponge pucks or tennis balls from the top at the blue line. Using sponge pucks or tennis balls in practice can help prevent injury.

Procedure
When a sponge puck or tennis ball is spotted in, the two forwards must work together to ensure that the puck does not get through to the net. The forward who is on the strong side must stay in the shooting lane and work to deny the shot. The backside forward must sag down a little bit with their stick on the inside to deter any seam passes. If the puck gets moved over to the other shooter, this backside forward must work to stay up in the shooting lane and the other forward must sag back. The

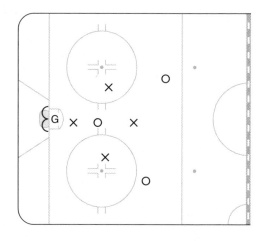

defense should stay off the forwards and be in a layer in the event the shot gets past the first layer. After the shot is blocked, the penalty-killing team must work to get to the loose sponge puck (or tennis ball) and shoot it down the ice. The offensive forward in front is looking to screen the goalie, deflect shots, and put pressure on the penalty killers if there is a loose puck. Their job is to get to the loose puck and get it back up to the point for another offensive shot. Points can be given for blocked shots (1 point for the defensive team), shots on goal (1 point for the offensive team), goal (2 points for the offensive team), and no shots for the full shift (2 points for the defensive team).

Coaching Tips

- This game is useful for team building because players will see the importance of blocking shots and taking opportunities away from the other team by being in the shooting lane. The game is good to play after the team has worked on shot blocking.
- Ensure that everyone rotates into the penalty-kill situation and remind players that real pucks will hurt a little more in games. Even so, players should never turn their backs to the puck where there is no protection.
- Remind players that they can block shots in three ways:
  1. Shin pads together—when the player has forward momentum and is in the lane. The player can keep gliding forward toward the shooter, using their stick either to take away a passing lane or to be at the toes if someone is shooting.
  2. Down on one knee—when the player does not have forward momentum and is in the shooting lane. The player can drop to one knee and have their stick in a passing lane.
  3. Sliding—useful as a last resort if the player is out of the shooting lane and needs to get back into the shooting lane. The player works on timing and tries to get the shin pads lined up with the puck when it is being shot. If possible, the player slides into the shooter's feet with the stick in a position to make themselves bigger if the opponent tries to stickhandle around them. Players should slide on their side so that the puck will hit them in their shin pads if they block it.

Variation

- An offensive player can be added as another shooter at the top to simulate flanks and a shooter at the top. This variation will start to get into more movement because your defense will have to step up to one of the flanks to be in the lane. The movement of the penalty killers is important, and they need to get to loose pucks first after they are blocked.

2 VS 2 WITH PLUS 1

Level of Difficulty
Hard

Minutes
10-12

Players
Full team

Objective
To teach players to read what is happening.

Setup
This game is played with nets placed at the bottom of the circle. A 2 vs 2 is played on each side of the imaginary middle line. One side is one team's offensive side, and the other side is their defensive side. The defensive side works to clear the puck to the offensive side.

Procedure
When the coach spots a puck, the defensive team tries to clear it to the offensive side and the offensive side tries to score. When the defensive team passes the puck to the offensive side of the game, a player can jump in to make it a 3 vs 2. The two defensive players have two offensive players waiting and try to clear the puck to them. If that happens, the player who jumped into the offensive side must quickly get back to play defense. A new defensive player can jump into the game and play on

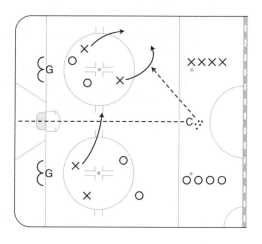

the offensive side, and the game goes back and forth. To keep things interesting, the offensive players can rotate with the defensive players, but only three players can be on one side of the imaginary line.

Coaching Tips
- Encourage players to move the puck quickly and jump into the lanes that are available. If they are standing behind someone else, they are not available to get a pass.
- Players should move without the puck to create passing lanes for their teammates.

3 VS 2 HALF ZONE

Level of Difficulty
Easy

Minutes
8-10

Players
Full team (half in each end)

Objectives
To work on a half-wall setup with puck possession, passing, and puck retrievals on loose pucks.

Setup
Three offensive players set up in the zone on one half wall. One player is on the half wall, one is down low, and one is in the slot. Two defensive players play either aggressively by putting pressure on the puck or passively by sitting. The coach spots in pucks.

Procedure
When the coach spots in the puck, the offensive team must work to get possession through passing and puck support. They must work the puck around to get it to the net without a player taking someone on 1 vs 1. They have support and should work to use it. Shifts can be 20 to 30 seconds long. As soon as the shift ends, the coach spots a puck to the other side, where another group is set up. The idea here is that the offensive team must read pressure and adjust accordingly.

Coaching Tips
- If there is pressure, the passes should be quick to support, and the players must move the puck away from pressure either behind the net, up the wall, or to the middle.
- Defensively, players should work together and communicate to minimize chances against them.

Variation
- If players are having trouble 3 vs 2, adjust the game to be 3 vs 1 to allow more space to move the puck.

BEHIND NET PASSING

Level of Difficulty

Easy

Minutes

6-8

Players

Five players with or without a goalie

Objective

To work on plays from below the goal line to the slot and to teach players to move offensively and have an active stick to deflect passes.

Setup

Have one player behind the net with a coach spotting pucks to them. Have two players in the slot offensively and two players defensively.

Procedure

When the coach spots the first puck to the player behind the net, the offensive players must move in the slot to become available. The defensive players work to keep pucks from the slot and deflect pucks away from the net. The coach spots five pucks into the small-area game and then rotates players around.

Coaching Tips

- Encourage the defensive players to have active sticks and poke pucks away.
- If a rebound comes to the front of the net, players can play the rebound.
- As a coach, you can make the initial spot of the puck more difficult or easier for the players. Direct passes are easy plays, and rims or pucks on the boards are more difficult plays.

Variation

- This small-area game can be moved into the neutral zone as a station for players or can be played in both ends with the net in the regular spot.

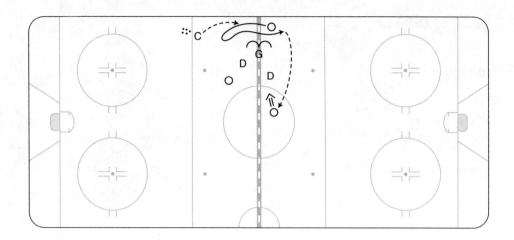

3 VS 2 HIGH

Level of Difficulty
Hard

Minutes
8-10

Players
Full team (half in each end)

Objective
To expose players to the top of a 1-3-1 power play where one-timers are used.

Setup
Three offensive players set up in the zone. One is on each side around the top of the circle, and one is in the middle at the blue line. Two defensive players line up in the slot ready to react to the puck as it moves.

Procedure
The puck is given to one of the offensive players, and they must work to get the puck to the net with a clean shot. The two defensive players work to steer the puck away from shooting lanes and block shots when necessary. The offensive team can move their feet to get into available passing lanes and should work to become available. The puck should move quickly and accurately to teammates who are looking to shoot.

Coaching Tips
- Offensive players can use wrist shots or slapshots to get the puck to the net, depending on the space provided to them.
- Defensively, players can have active sticks and should recognize who they are against and where the shooting lanes come from.

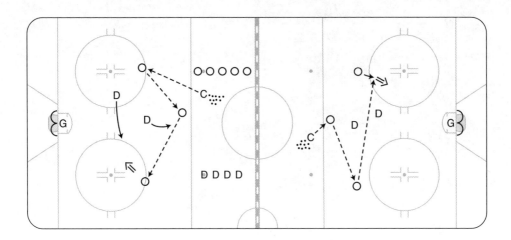

CHAPTER 6

Transition Games

This chapter helps coaches challenge players to begin thinking in a game setting. Players must think and react quickly because they will be transitioning from defense to offense and from offense to defense. They must be able to skate as well as work on and execute small-area skills both with and without the puck to be successful in the games. Players off the puck are important because the puck carrier needs support options; each player must move and become available as the games play out. Using transition games in practice is an effective way to ensure that players can work and execute skills under pressure.

Here are some of the areas that are important for using transition games effectively in practice.

SKATING

The key to good transitions with the puck is having players in the right spots to disrupt puck possession from the offensive team. Good skating and a good understanding of time and space make this possible. Good checking habits come from good angles, good stick position, and good gap control to work to take away available space. Typically, when I work with young players who are not confident in their skating, they allow a bigger gap so that they do not get beat. I would prefer to have players get beat in practice from trying to establish a proper gap instead of sitting back and allowing the attacking player time and space to create something offensively. I often see coaches get upset with players for getting beat, but if those players do not learn in practice through failing, they may never be in the right position in games. When players have confidence in their skating, you will see them work on their edges to take away time and space and force opponents into space where they want them to go. This ability to angle and steer creates turnovers through contact and support, which allows players to get into transition situations with the puck. The ability to react quickly either to turn the puck with a strong tight turn and accelerate in the other direction or change directions to support the puck requires good balance and good skating.

ANGLING

Angling is the ability to steer someone in the desired direction and take away their time and space. Good angling skills are directly related to good skating skills. Players need to be able to come from underneath the puck to ensure that the puck carrier does not have the option to cut back behind them. This ability comes from taking the necessary ice and adjusting their route to skate with the puck carrier and run them out of space. In practice, players of all ages struggle with taking proper angles and recognizing the attacking players' speed. Continue to work with players and give them reps in the drill to help them learn. In games, players must remember that they will have support. Their ability to angle and steer can move the puck carrier into a location on the ice where the defending team is stronger, perhaps where another defender is waiting to help, or where the puck carrier is in a less dangerous position. A good practice option is to progress simple 1 vs 1 angling drills to allow the defensive players to steer the offensive forward into another defender.

PUCK MOVEMENT

When turnovers are created, the defending team (or players) can quickly work to begin attacking on the offensive side again. In games, to cover space quickly, puck movement can be used to catch teams that turned over the puck. A key part of having a successful transition game is that the player who picks up the loose puck must have an option to move the puck to. Therefore, the players off the puck must work to get open to create options. Depending on the situation in games or practice, you should teach players to move the puck when they are supposed to, not when they have to. By moving the puck the other way quickly, transitions can be a key part to success in games. Transitions can be developed from drills and then added into small-area games that focus on checking, takeaways, and puck transitions to go from defense to offense. Transition games really encourage players to work on all areas of their skating. There are times when players will move forward, times when they will move backward, and times when they will need to transition from one to the other. At other times they will have to work against another player in a confined space with two feet on the ice to battle for pucks. The result of this type of small-area game is having players who can react to what they see happening on the ice.

PUCK SUPPORT

Building on puck movement is a requirement to having players support the puck when they do not have it. Supporting the puck can occur in different areas and is largely based on how much help a teammate needs. Players can choose to be in close support when a battle for the puck is occurring because the player battling can then simply bump the puck to available space where the support player can pick it up. By working on this concept in small-area games, players learn to find where their help is and can move the puck to space for them to gain possession. This situation comes up in games in the corners and along the walls. Teams can maintain possession without the risk of throwing long, rink-wide passes to the closest available player. By having close support, the puck can be moved to available space quickly and then turned to go the other way.

Support can also come in the form of covering more space quickly through good recognition of available space. This situation can occur when pucks that are chipped in the neutral zone do not get as deep as they were intended to. Players off the puck may find that they have an opportunity to change directions quickly with more of a stretch pass that covers distance. By recognizing this type of support, teams that can support and move the puck quickly can make opponents pay for turning over the puck. Small-area games that involve quick transitions and puck movement build support options into players' minds so that they can use them in games. Keep in mind that as players become more aware of their involvement in the play, you can challenge them to use multiple passes to launch quick strikes the other way.

PUCK PROTECTION

The offensive side of puck possession is puck protection, which ensures that transitions are harder to come by. I ask players, "Where should the puck be when you are playing against other players?" The answer I look for from players is "protected." Having the puck protected maintains possession and the opportunity to advance it. When we work on this with players, we call it "puck location" because we want players to think about where they are putting the puck based on their situation. With no pressure, they can put it in a spot wherever they want to make a play. If there is pressure, they should understand that the movement of the puck needs to be to a protected position. At high levels, if players put the puck in the wrong spot, it will be gone in transition. Understanding puck location is a key part of developing puck skills after players have acquired the fundamentals of stickhandling. After they build confidence with the puck, they need to work on reacting to move the puck away from pressure.

One area that comes up with puck protection occurs when players cross their hands over, thinking they are protecting the puck. But this position creates a weaker stick by bringing the puck back closer to checkers. In addition, players cannot make a play from that position with their hands. Instead of crossing their hands over on the forehand side, players should simply move their top hand to their outside hip (right-handed players move their left hand to the right hip and left-handed players move their left hand to the right hip) and not allow their top hand to be outside their bottom hand on their stick. This position creates better separation for the puck carrier because they can use their body to build a wall between themselves and the checker. Moreover, they can do something with the puck. If they cross their hands, they will need to reset them to make a play. From the recommended position, players can make a play quicker when they see a play developing.

STEALS AND TAKEAWAYS

The defensive side of transitioning the puck involves teaching players how to take the puck away from an attacking forward. The goal of the defensive player is to disrupt clean possession of the puck and create a loose puck that either they or a teammate can get and start it going back the other way. Through good angling skills, players can create a good body position and take away space. At some point, the stick will go from a steering position to a checking position that will go stick to puck. Here are a couple of ways to work on steals and takeaways.

Stick Lift

With good body position and seeing the exposed puck, the defensive player comes from a half step behind the puck carrier. The player comes under the puck carrier's stick, aiming close to the heel of their stick, popping it up, and coming back to the puck. The player must not lift too close to their hands because a penalty may be called if the stick gets horizontal to the ice. The movement to pop the stick must be quick and come right back to the puck. If the positioning is right from the angling, the defender can place their hips to the offensive player's hands to box them out away from the puck as they are lifting the stick. The timing of the stick lift and hip position will ensure that the dispossessed player is left behind as the puck is transitioned the other way.

Stick Extend

By extending the stick to its full reach, the defensive player appears bigger. A caution here is to avoid overextending to a point where the stick becomes weak. Players cannot skate in this position for long, but it is useful when used properly. The poke at the puck can knock the puck forward to a supporting player. This movement should be fast and direct to the puck. If the player misses the puck with the poke, they can pull the stick back quickly and get it to the puck on the way back. Venla Hovi (three-time Finnish Olympian and now coach) calls this technique the "snake's tongue," a name that always made me smile. These methods work well if the defensive player is coming from behind the puck and the puck is exposed. I also work with players on the situation when they cannot get access to the puck. They simply get their stick under the puck carrier's stick (even with one hand) and keep skating. If the defensive player can lift their stick while under the attacking forward's stick, they can often create separation between the blade and the puck, possibly causing a turnover and a transition opportunity.

Stick Down

By keeping the stick down, the defensive player is simply working to take away a passing lane if their angle will not get them close enough to the puck to get their stick to it. By placing the stick down quickly, the player can block the lane and possibly intercept or deflect the pass. This play is common near the offensive blue line with passes coming from the outside toward the middle or in tight to the net with passes coming from below the goal line to the net. This situation is based on the space available and not being able to get close enough to go stick to puck. Defensively, the player is trying to create an obstacle that requires the puck carrier to adjust or elevate their pass.

TRANSITION GAMES

Small-area games can be effective in training players to process information that is happening in front of them. Transition games require players to be aware of their surroundings so that they can quickly transition the puck the other way. The objective is to capitalize on a turnover. Several options can be used in transition games.

Pass to a Coach

Including the coaches is a great way to have players use one end and keep up the pace of the game. This scheme means that the players on defense must pass to a waiting coach to transition from defense to offense; the coach passes it back to the team who passed to them. The coaches can rotate around the zone, or several coaches can be used as transition passing options. Using a smaller zone (one zone or top of the circle down) can create a fast game with changes of possession and quick chances to the net.

Pass to a Teammate in the Game

Players must make one pass to a teammate and then go on offense. The pace of the game is fast, which encourages players to work for a quick-strike offense.

Pass to the Line of Players Who Are Waiting to Change Possession

This adjustment keeps more players involved as they are resting. Players can be on the side of the game in a line to create a boundary, so those playing know exactly where support is.

Shift Players

Games can have rotations of players like line changes in a game. Having players go from offense to defense or defense to offense is a good way to have players play when they are a little tired.

Small-area games can benefit the transition game because players must think and react quickly. The goalies will be busy because the game should be fast with quick support, quick passes, and quick-strike offense from one end to the other. By changing the games being played, coaches can choose the skills to be included in the games. Scoring can be as simple as awarding points for goals, but scoring can also include steals and takeaways or transition passes off turnovers. These changes can encourage players to focus on the topics of the session and work to try them more in competitive situations.

PASS TO SUPPORT

Level of Difficulty
Easy

Minutes
8-10

Players
Small group to full team

Objectives
To work on puck movement and always knowing where the supporting player is.

Setup
Play this game in a confined area. Start with a 1 vs 1 and a supporting player for each player in the game.

Procedure
When the puck is spotted in, both players work to win the battle for the puck and pass to their support player before they can attempt to score. The defensive team must get the puck back and then work to get into available ice to get the puck back to score. What makes this game tricky is that the supporting player is constantly moving, so the players in the game must be aware of what is happening around them. Each shift can last 20 to 30 seconds. The coach then spots a new puck for new players. The rotation can be support player, player in game, rest.

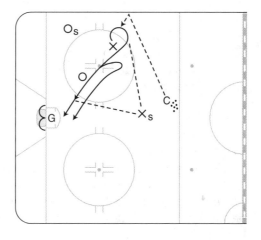

Coaching Tip
- The key to this game is communication from the support player to the player in the game. When the player in the game knows where the supporting player is, they can move the puck quicker.

Variations
- This game can be played in the full zone, on one side of the offensive zone, or even cross ice. Players must always be aware of their surroundings.

PASSING FOR POINTS

Level of Difficulty
Moderate

Minutes
10-15

Players
12-18

Objectives
To build on passing, pass-receiving skills, and spatial awareness. To stress puck support and continued movement to help players see success in the game.

Setup
This game is played in one end zone. Divide teams into two sides, distinguished by color of jersey. Set up cones (or tires) roughly two stick lengths apart to create three gates. One gate is at the top of the zone in the middle, and the other two gates are in the face-off circles parallel to the boards. The net can be left in place or removed, but there is no shooting in this game. The game works best when played 3 vs 3 because players have multiple options to pass the puck to. This game does not include a goalie, so it is best used when the goalie is working with a goalie coach.

Procedure
The players earn a point in this game every time they pass the puck successfully to a teammate through a gate. The game transitions from offense to defense quickly because as soon as the puck is turned over, players can react and try to score points for their team. The coach can control shift length by having players change on the whistle. Players will have to be responsible defensively because the team with the puck can score multiple points quickly (by passing back and forth by one-touching the puck). The offensive team (team with the puck) should look to move the puck quickly and then move to open space to be available to get the puck back.

Coaching Tips
- The game focuses on the players off the puck providing multiple passing options to the player with the puck. As players become better at the game, they will start to learn how to move to available space.
- When learning to play this game, players will try to get points on every pass. As they improve, they will learn to move the puck a lot and then pass.

- Defensively, this game helps players learn to react to what is happening and to communicate constantly and adapt. Defensive players can focus on taking away time and space quickly to make it harder for the offensive team to make successful passes. Defensive players can also focus on good stick positions to break up passes or force more difficult passes.

Variations

- The game can be played 2 vs 2 if you have a smaller group, but it becomes harder because only one option is available. In this case, a coach can jump in to be a passing option. A coach can play for each team, or a single coach can be an additional outlet for both teams. Pucks can be spotted in or rimmed in to challenge players to work on wall battles and pulling the puck off the wall after handling a rim under pressure.

- If the group is at a high level, a useful variation is to have players change on their own but only when their team is on offense. This rule encourages good changes and reinforces the importance of puck possession in allowing players to change in the offensive zone and establish sustained time in the offensive zone.

- If you have a goaltender in net, you can have players pass the puck through a set of tires to go on offense before they try to score.

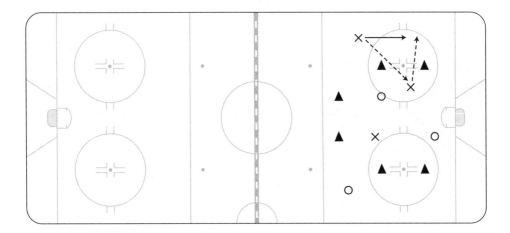

TWO NET—READ THE PLAY

Level of Difficulty
Moderate

Minutes
10-15

Players
Full team

Objectives
To start to see open ice and read available ice when the puck is transitioned from offense to defense or defense to offense.

Setup
Set up one net on the goal line in its normal spot and the other on the top of the circle, both facing out toward the coach, who has pucks at the blue line. Divide the group into two teams. They play either 2 vs 2 or 3 vs 3, depending on the number of players on each team.

Procedure
When the coach dumps a puck in, the two (or three) players work to find it. They must make one pass to a teammate before they can score. The offensive team can score on either net. The offensive players should look to get to the net quickly whenever they have a chance to score. This game helps to create an offensive instinct to score more goals. If the defensive team gets possession of the puck, they must make one pass to a teammate before they can score. The coach can control the shift length to 30 to 45 seconds to keep the tempo of the game high.

Coaching Tip
- This game is beneficial because it works on puck movement, player movement, shot selection, plays behind the net for the goalies, and more. Encourage players to think quickly and start to read where players will be going. When players start to defend the space they think offensive players will move to, the offensive team has to work to new available ice.

Variation

- This game can be played with players passing to each other to change the offensive team, or it can be played with players passing to a coach on each side. Allowing players to pass to a coach works well when the game is being played 2 vs 2 because the offensive team has more options to move the puck to. This variation can be done with two coaches (one on each side of the ice). When they receive a pass from the defensive team, they pass it back to a player on the defensive team, which then becomes the offensive team. The coaches can move around the zone so that the defensive players must have their heads up to find the available coach to move the puck to.

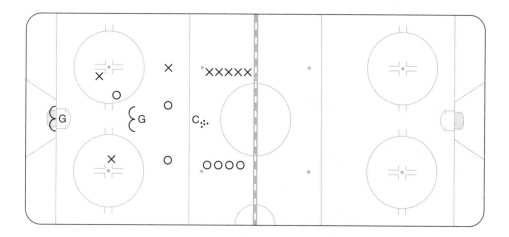

3 VS 3 CROSS ICE

Level of Difficulty
Easy to Hard

Minutes
10-15

Players
Full team

Objectives
To work on supporting the puck, moving the puck, and transitioning the puck from defense to offense quickly.

Setup
Place nets in the zone across the ice from each other. The zone is the playing area.

Procedures
Players play 3 vs 3 and work to score on the other net. They play 30 to 45 seconds per shift. A coach can spot a new puck into the zone for each group, or the players can continue to play the puck from the previous group. Also, the coach spots in a new puck if the puck leaves the zone for any reason. Encourage players to transition to offense quickly when they get the puck.

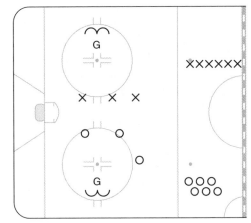

Coaching Tips
- These games move quickly, so playing the game to 3 or 5 is a good way to allow players to play to win.
- Encourage players to control the puck and move it when they have the chance to do so.
- Taking players on 1 vs 1 is a high-risk play that may cause loss of possession of the puck and a quick transition for the other team.

Variations
This type of 3 vs 3 game can be played with many variations that are effective in addressing specific areas of the game that your team needs to work on. Here are some of the variations I have found useful:

- Pass to the coach to line change (hard). This variation allows the team with the puck to change and holds the defensive team on the ice. You usually do this to reinforce to the players that they cannot change when the puck is in their end of the ice. This game encourages the players to work to get possession and then change when they get the puck. This advanced option is best with experienced groups who understand the benefit of making line changes on the offensive side of the play.

- Start 2 vs 2 and add a player—angling (hard). To add a player, the team must pass back to their line. The new player coming in must skate the puck behind the net, allowing the defensive team to establish an angle to where the player is going. When the player comes out on the other side of the net, they should be in a position where they need to move the puck to a teammate. If the defending team fails to establish an angle on this player, the offensive player can keep skating. This game can be played up to 3 vs 3; in that case, two new players would start another shift. This variation is especially useful after a day of working on angling.

- Increase the value of goals for what you worked on (easy). For example, if you were teaching deflections or rebounds for the day, those types of goals would be worth 2 points. This scoring bonus will encourage players to work on scoring those types of goals in the game. If you worked on passing, you can say that the point value of a goal is equal to the number of passes that led to the goal. Players will then work to pass the puck more.

- Play your 3 vs 3 game to 1 and put something on the line for the team that gets scored on (easy). Typically, when I do this, I play for one down-and-back each game. The punishment for getting scored on adds an incentive and magnifies the little errors. Players will start to compete a little harder each shift when they know that every goal has a consequence.

- 3 vs 3 with a defensive breakout player below the net. This player is responsible for transitioning the puck from defense to offense any time they get it. When the defending team creates a turnover, they must move the puck behind their net and then work to support the puck. This option adds another player and forces players to work to become available for a pass. When the coach changes the players, the player from behind the net area is one of the players who jumps into the game along with two others from the bench.

- 3 vs 3 with a third man high. This game promotes awareness from the offensive team to always have an option above the puck. They need to be able to see the play and scan the ice to have someone above the halfway line. The high player can rotate into the offensive zone if someone takes them out. By having only two offensive players near the net, the defensive team can outnumber the offensive team on the puck while taking away time, space, and passing lanes. When the puck transitions to the other team, they can have only two players go on offense to try to score, with one player remaining high. This game creates odd-number rushes on quick transitions but also teaches players to be patient when their team is on offense.

1 VS 1 WITH HELP COMING

Level of Difficulty
Hard

Minutes
10-15

Players
Full team

Objectives
To work on angles, communication, and puck support.

Setup
This game is played cross ice with a goalie in each net. Divide the players to have the same number on each team. The coach has pucks in the middle of the zone at the blue line. One player from each side starts the game.

Procedure
The coach starts the game by dumping the puck to one side to give offensive possession to one player. The other player has to angle that player. They play 1 vs 1; the offensive player tries to score, and the defensive player tries to deny any high-percentage chances to the net. After they cross center, the coach gives the defensive team another player to help. This player must communicate with the defensive player on the puck. When this player gets the puck, they take it the other way, and a new player from the other team works to angle the puck carrier. When the puck gets past center, the coach gives the defensive team a new player. Players should rotate around so that they become the angling defensive player and the supporting defensive player on different shifts. The line changes happen quickly and by themselves: defense, offense, rest.

Coaching Tip
- In this quick transition game, players must be ready to jump in to angle and steer the offensive team into a position where they can be controlled. If you have to switch sides, you can do this midgame so that players can angle the other way.

Variation

- This game can also be played as a 2 vs 2 or 3 vs 3 game. The biggest difference is that the new group must angle the attacking team so that the group coming off the bench is starting on defense and must work to regain possession of the puck. As soon as they get possession, they should transition the puck from defense to offense quickly because two (or three) new players from the other team are coming in to play defense and are working to establish a good angle. This game requires a high level of puck support and puck possession. One simple rule is that the puck must cross over center before a change of possession can take place and new or different players are added off the bench.

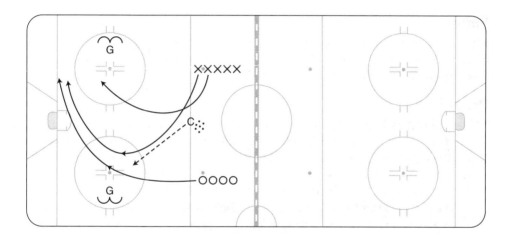

3 VS 3 ANGLE

Level of Difficulty
Hard

Minutes
10-15

Players
Full team

Objectives
To work on angling opposing players and steering them in the desired direction. The goal of this game is to have players realize that they are angling so that teammates can read where the puck is going to go.

Setup
Place nets in the zone across the ice from each other. The zone is the playing area. With pucks in the middle of the blue line, the coach can distribute them into the game or throw a new one into the game.

Procedure
Players play 3 vs 3 and work to score on the other net. The coach starts each shift by spotting a puck to one side (the other side gets the next puck). One of the three players grabs the puck and skates behind their own net. They cannot stop behind the net and must continue out the other side. The other two offensive players work to get open for the puck carrier. The defensive team must work to angle the puck carrier to keep going down the wall or where the players behind the first player can read where the puck is going and work to get a turnover. The shift continues with 3 vs 3 play. On the whistle the next 3 vs 3 shift starts. The coach spots a puck to the opposite team, and the group that is finished brings their puck out of the zone.

Coaching Tips
- Encourage players to start the shift quickly by getting across and angling the player who is coming behind the net and not allowing them to cut back into the middle of the ice.
- The two other players behind the first forechecking player must read the play and move according to where the puck could go. A key part to the game is that players must move and read the play so that three players are not going to the puck or the player skating up the ice, leaving players open.
- The coaches can flip the group halfway through the game or play the game a second day with the players on opposite sides so that they are angling the opposite way.

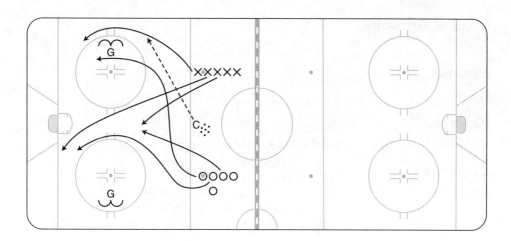

PASS TO COACH

Level of Difficulty
Easy

Minutes
10-15

Players
Full team (can be played in one end or both ends)

Objectives
This quick defense-to-offense transition game can be played in each end to maximize playing time for each group or in one end if the group is smaller. Players can focus on moving the puck quickly with good passing skills and movement off the puck.

Setup
Coaches have pucks at the blue line in the middle with two teams, one on each side of them. The extra coaches can be spread out around the zone on the half wall or at the blue line. The game has one goalie, and the net is set up in the regular spot.

Procedure
The game starts with a coach spotting the puck into the zone and three players from each team coming into the end zone. Whichever team gets the puck first must pass to a coach and then work to get open to get it back. Any player on the team that passed to the coach can get it back before that team tries to score. The defensive team must work to get possession of the puck and then pass to any coach before their team can work to score. A coach controls the shift length with a whistle that signals the next shift to start.

Coaching Tips
- This game of quick transitions requires players to change from defense to offense and back to defense multiple times.
- Players must work to get open on offense and move to become available to receive a pass from a coach.

Variation
- Have the coaches move around midshift so that they are not always posted up in the same spot where the players know exactly where they are. Having the players look for the coaches will make passing harder, so more missed passes will result. This variation is useful after you have played the game a couple of times and want to challenge the players with something new.

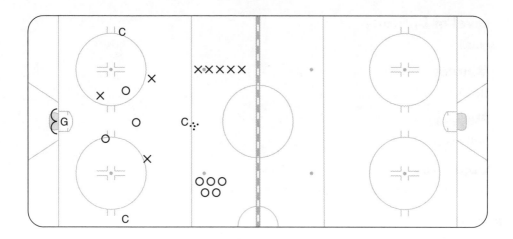

3 VS 3 WITH LOW PLAYER

Level of Difficulty
Hard

Minutes
10-15

Players
Full team

Objectives
To work on quick plays from below the goal line to the slot.

Setup
The group plays 3 vs 3. A coach is in the middle of the group with pucks. Place the nets across the ice from each other with a goalie in each net. Behind each net is one player from the offensive team during each shift.

Procedure
The game starts 3 vs 3 with either a face-off or a spotted puck. After one team gains possession of the puck, they must pass or rim the puck to the player behind the net, who must control the puck and move it to a player attacking the net. The defensive team must work to get possession of the puck and move it to their player down low to score. When a line change occurs, the player who was below the goal line is one of the players who moves into the next shift and a new player replaces them.

Coaching Tip
- This game works best when the player below the net is active in the play and moves to support the puck. They do not have to just stand behind the net; they can move out either side. Encourage them to move the puck as soon as they see a passing lane because they may have a chance to catch the other team on the transition.

Variation
- This game can be played with the offensive team having two players down low behind the net who can pass to each other. This additional player makes passing more of an option than skating.

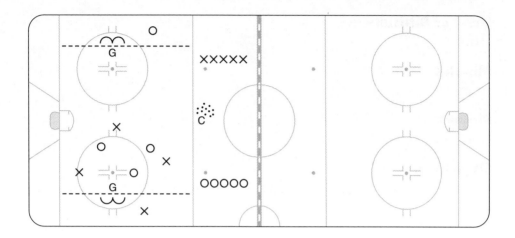

2 VS 1 IN ZONE

Level of Difficulty
Hard

Minutes
10-12

Players
Full team

Objectives
To work transitioning the puck quickly and jumping up in the play to create a 2 vs 1.

Setup
Place nets across the ice from each other. One player starts with the puck in their defensive zone. They have a teammate waiting for them in the other zone (across the midline of the ice), and a defensive player waits there as well. The player with the puck jumps in to make it a 2 vs 1 in the offensive zone.

Procedure
The play goes for 10 to 15 seconds, and if the defensive player can get the puck, they transition it the other way. If they cannot get the puck, the coach spots them a transition puck and they jump up to make it a 2 vs 1 going the other way. A new defensive player plays the 2 vs 1 each shift to start their shift. They play defense and then offense twice before rotating out.

Coaching Tip
- In this quick transition game, players must be aware of what is happening around them on the ice. They must be ready to defend and then quickly jump on offense to work to make something happen.

Variation
- After players get the hang of the 2 vs 1 games, they can play it as a 2 vs 2 transition game. Players play defense, then offense, and then rotate out.

ONE PLAYER IN BOX

Level of Difficulty
Hard

Minutes
10-12

Players
Full team (half in each end)

Objectives
To develop awareness and get pucks to the front of the net where goals can be scored.

Setup
Three players from each team are in the zone. Set up a box in the slot. Only one player can be in the boxed area if the puck is not there as well. Coaches spread out in the zone for the players to move the puck to before a team goes on offense.

Procedure
The puck is spotted to one team. Two players move the puck around, and one player stays in the slot area (where the box is). If the puck goes into the box, all three players can go into the box and work to score. The defensive team tries to get possession of the puck and pass it to a coach, who passes it back so that they can attempt to score. There are no rules for where the defensive team can stand against the offensive team. Shift length is roughly 30 seconds. The coach then changes the players in the game.

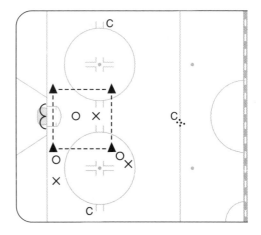

Coaching Tips
- Encourage your players to move in and out of the box, constantly changing to create available lanes to the net while remembering that only one player can be in the box when the puck is not near the net.
- When the defensive team gets possession of the puck and moves it to the coach, they must work to get available in a place where there is a passing lane.

CHAPTER 7

Face-Off Games

Face-offs are one of the most interesting parts of the game for me because as a group, five (or six) of your players are trying to win possession of the puck for your team. After you have possession, you are trying to make something happen either by executing a set play off your draw or by reacting to what you see (or both). In either case, what you do after you win the face-off will help your team either clear the zone, enter the zone, or create possession or a chance in the offensive zone. Having players work through what to do on face-offs is a key for the success of any team in games. You can do this work through on-ice practice, through boardroom meetings, through video review, or through all three. After players understand what they are doing in games and where they will stand, they can make a better play or get to the puck first. You can practice those ideas first and then use them in a small-area game.

THE WHO, WHAT, AND WHERE OF FACE-OFFS

As players are taking face-offs in games, they need to be aware of several things before they take the draw. By having an idea of all those things (which they should be able to take in quickly), they will be able to make a good decision about what they are going to do to win the face-off as an individual or as a group.

Who Is on the Ice?

By knowing who is on the ice for the other team, players may choose to take more or fewer risks on the face-off. Your team does not want to make a high-risk play when the other team's best players are on the ice; they want to avoid giving skilled opponents possession of the puck. Being able to recognize quickly who they are out against will allow your team to decide as a group what they are going to do on the face-off to win possession.

What Zone Is the Face-Off In?

Knowing which zone (offensive, neutral, or defensive zone) the face-off is in will help players recognize what they may have to do to win the draw. Generally, the rule in the defensive zone is that the center does not have to win the draw; they just cannot lose the draw clean. That result means that every puck in the defensive zone will be either scrambled, tied up, or won back by the defense. The one thing you do not want to happen is for the other team to win the draw clean and be able to create a scoring chance. The neutral zone is where players can work to win the face-off in a variety of ways to gain possession of the puck. The offensive zone is where your team can work to beat the opposing center as they work through the mentality of not losing the draw. Players may be able to get creative by going forward on the draw toward the net, or they may work to pull the puck back to the defense. In any case, you have multiple options about how you can win the draw. If you can win the draw back clean to your defense, your team should have the option to run a set play to create a chance to the net.

What Side of the Ice Is the Face-Off On?

Knowing what side of the ice the draw is on will help players quickly recognize situations in the moment of the game. Before getting set for the face-off, the center should talk to their teammates beforehand to ensure that everyone is on the same page. Most players are stronger at winning the puck to the backhand side of the body because the motion to win the draw is easier compared with the motion on their forehand side. Most teams have both right-handed centers and left-handed centers for the different sides of the ice.

What Is the Game Situation?

By being able to recognize the situation in the game quickly, the center will know how risky they can be. Is the face-off even strength, a power play, a penalty kill, or an end-of-game situation that includes an extra attacker either for or against? Recognizing this situation may put extra pressure on specific face-offs in games, but that intensity at the competitive level leads to great moments.

What Is the Score in the Game?

Is your team down by one, in which case you are pushing for a goal and your forwards need to win possession of the puck? Is your team up by one, in which case your team is protecting the lead? The decision that your players make on the draw could mean the difference between winning and losing. Either way, on the way to the face-off circle, your players should look at the scoreboard to confirm what is happening in the game at that exact moment.

What Is the Other Center Trying to Do With the Face-Off?

The opposing center may give away their intentions as they approach the circle for the face-off. Is their bottom hand turned over? How are their feet positioned? Do they have a shooter behind them? Are they running a set play that your team has seen before, or are they coming to tie up your players? A center who can pick up cues in the face-off circle will likely have more success on face-offs in games. Some centers resort to doing the same thing every time, and a player who can get a read on what they are doing can have good success against them.

What Is the Alignment of the Other Team and Are They Trying to Run Something Quickly if They Can Win the Face-Off?

In the offensive zone, teams often try to create an offensive chance if they can win the face-off. They can adjust the alignment of their wingers to drop someone back behind the center, they can shift their defense over to make it harder for coverage, or they can have set movements if they win the draw clean to work to open something up toward the net. The center needs to be aware of all these possibilities; they do not want to lose the draw in the defensive zone.

You as the coach will set up the alignment of players in practice, and the players who are on the ice for each face-off will execute it. Each player has a role on the face-off, and if they do their job correctly, your chances of winning the draw go up.

CENTER'S ROLE

The center takes the face-off and should be the last player who is set and ready to go for the face-off. Every other player on the ice should be ready for the draw before the center comes into the face-off circle. The center takes a wide stance and hinges at the waist to put the upper body over the face-off circle. This positioning allows the center to get over top of the dot quickly when the puck comes in and creates a battle for the puck with the other player. The center must find a stance that works for them on both sides of the ice and against various other players. What works against one player may not work against another player, and a center who can recognize that is one step ahead of the competition. The center has three main ways to win the draw, and each category has several options within it.

Straight Speed

With their eyes watching the ref's hand, as soon as the puck comes out, the center reacts and makes a quick movement to the puck. The movement to get their stick to the puck is fast and efficient. They are not worried about what the other center is trying to do. They focus only on being explosive and quick to ensure that they touch the puck first. The movement of the stick is fast and not so big that the other center can get inside and get to the puck first. The center can slide their hands down the stick to improve leverage and possibly turn their bottom hand over to help them win the draw back using straight speed.

Opponent's Stick First

As the ref drops the puck, the first motion of the center is to the opponent's stick to interrupt their path to winning the draw back to their side. The center then comes back to the puck. The contact with the opponent's stick should be done quickly and effectively to get the inside position coming back to the puck. When the center has inside position on the puck, if the opponent is stronger and pushes the stick back, the center will be the first to get to the puck. Each player who the center faces in a face-off is different, but the goal for contact on the opponent's stick is to aim the blade of the stick to meet the shaft of the opponent's stick and then come back to the puck. This technique can be very effective when done properly.

Tie Up the Face-Off

Players need to discuss this option before the puck is dropped so that the wingers are ready to jump in and help win possession of the puck back to the D. The first movement of the center when the puck comes into the circle is to tie up the opponent's stick and not allow them access to the puck. The center can do this by stepping forward into the opponent or by turning the hips into them. Either way, the center is not allowing the other center access to the puck. This way of winning the draw is not allowed in Europe or in any IIHF event, so players must become competent at the first two ways if they are playing in those regions or events.

Ultimately, the center has the job of ensuring that everyone is ready for the draw and prepared to help win possession of the puck. They do this by communicating before the draw so that everyone is on the same page with either a set play or just working to win possession of the puck. This communication can be tricky because you do not want the other team to hear you. Therefore, teams often communicate about what is happening on the way to the face-off circle or on the bench before coming on the ice. Teams may have words or phrases to describe a certain play so that when it is called, the other team does not know what is coming should your team win the face-off clean.

WINGER'S ROLE

The winger's job is to help on the draw before getting into their assignment off the draw. The first step should be toward the face-off dot if the winger is lining up in a spot where this can happen. In the defensive zone, one winger can help on the draw while the other lines up outside the dot. Daniel Tkaczuk calls these "edge battles," and a winger who can help the center win a draw gets a lot of additional ice time toward the end of the game or on important face-offs. In practice, players can work on being strong on the stick and using their position against the opponent to win a battle for the puck. Wingers will not have the boards to assist, so they must be able to get good positioning and recognize what is happening around them so that they can help the center win possession of the puck. A winger must also be able to take face-offs if the center is kicked out of the draw. The winger should be able to prevent the other team from winning the draw clean.

ZONE POSITIONS

In the offensive zone and neutral zone, the defense lines up back to support the puck and be the player who can make something happen with the puck when the draw is won back. This comes from practice and recognition of the situation in the game. In the defensive zone, players can line up closer to the face-off and be ready to help win the draw on the edge battle should the puck come their way. The defense lines up right beside a player from the other team on the boards, and winning possession of the puck can help ensure that nothing comes to the net quickly. Defensive players should practice taking some draws as well because if the team is killing a penalty 5 vs 3 and the center is kicked out of the face-off, the defensive player will have a chance to win the draw in that key moment in the game.

As a coach, in practice you should work through where everyone stands (in the defensive zone, neutral zone, and offensive zone) and what is happening should your team lose the draw or win the draw. Having everyone understand what they are doing is crucial in these key situations. When players know where they are going and what their job is on the draw, they form a cohesive unit on the ice that is hard to beat even if the opposing team wins the draw. Players should be able to react quickly and adjust when they recognize what is happening in the situation.

Practicing face-offs is a key part of practice because many face-offs occur in a game. If your team can be above the 60 to 70 percent mark, they are doing a good job winning draws. This number is high, but you should push to get there rather than be stuck aiming for 50 percent. Have the forwards work in small groups on specific areas of the face-off and then add the other players to make the situations for the face-off more competitive. You can work on stick movement with the players off the ice or watch video, but much of the work for draws is best done on the ice before or after practice or at a neutral-zone station where the forwards can get in some extra work without taking time away from other important areas.

When you are using face-offs as a key part to the practice, any small-area game you play at the end of the practice can have a face-off added in to start the shift. Adding a face-off into a 3 vs 3 down low immediately adds a starting element that is like a game and requires players to react to a won or lost face-off. This simple addition gives players more reps on face-offs, and as a coach you will see which players on your team are the best at taking face-offs and helping to win face-offs. You will have a good idea who should be on the ice when the time comes in a game.

FACE-OFF PRACTICE

Level of Difficulty
Easy

Minutes
6-8

Players
Forwards and possibly defensive players

Objectives
To have the centers and wingers take draws against each other. The goal is to help players feel comfortable taking draws against both right- and left-handed players.

Setup
Players can work in a group of three. One player drops pucks, and the other two take draws. If this is being done at the end of practice, a coach can drop pucks for the players when you have a couple minutes to focus on something specifically. Usually, it is better to have the players dropping pucks so that the coach can watch and make adjustments with players rather than focus on avoiding being hit.

Procedure
Have the player dropping the puck ensure that both players are ready to go and come in quickly. After the puck is dropped, the battle to win the puck is on. The player who wins the best of seven (must win four face-offs) stays in the face-off circle and goes against the next player. Keep rotating players around after they lose so that they go against a new player the next time.

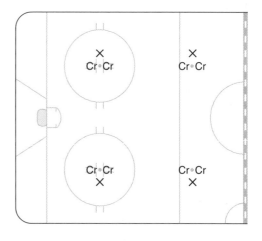

Coaching Tip
- Encourage players to focus on different ways to win the draw against different-hand players and work to recognize what the other center is trying to do to win the draw. When players know what the opponent is trying to do, winning the draw becomes easier.

Variation
- Add more players to make this activity more like a face-off in a game.

EDGE BATTLE

Level of Difficulty
Easy

Minutes
6-8

Players
Forwards (and possibly defensive players)

Objectives
To work on winning back pucks that were tied up by the center on face-offs.

Setup
Players line up on each side of the face-off circle as they would in a game. The coach is in the middle on the face-off dot.

Procedure
The coach drops a puck toward the players lined up on one side of the hash marks. They both try to win possession of the puck for their team by getting the puck back onto their side of the ice. After one battle, the coach turns around and drops a puck the other way for the players on the that side. This turning and dropping for the other group allows players to get set after a quick break and take the next puck that comes their way. Players should keep in mind that not every puck is going to come to them in a game.

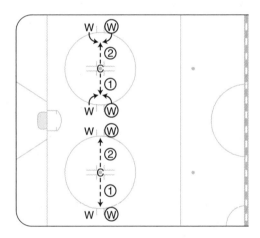

Coaching Tip
- Have the players be prepared to be strong on their sticks and work to get inside position on the opponent. The concept "position before possession" is useful here; players need to think about how they are working against another player to get the puck for their team. All they need to do is bump the puck to an area where the next player can move the puck either by skating it, passing it, or shooting it down the ice (if killing a penalty).

Variation
- Add a second player to the inside of the defensive-zone draw to represent a defense on the face-off as well.

WIN THE PUCK

Level of Difficulty

Moderate

Minutes

6-8

Players

Full team

Objectives

To create a battle for the puck on face-offs to win the puck back to an area.

Setup

Players work in a group of three to take two draws each. The other two players line up in a position on the outside of the circle, waiting to win the edge battle. Place a pad at the bottom of the circle behind each group of three players.

Procedure

With a coach (or another player) dropping the puck, the players come into the face-off circle as they do in a game. One player takes the draw, and one player on each side of them is ready to help should the puck go that way. The game is short and quick as players battle to get each puck dropped back to the area behind them and hit the pad. Each time the puck hits the pad, that team gets 1 point. Keep track of the points won by each team and have something for the winners.

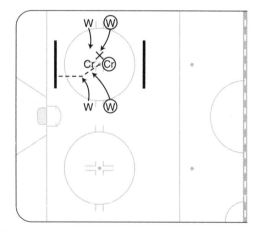

Coaching Tips

- This game is useful when players are playing another game in the other end or when no goalies are available because there is no shooting.
- With multiple players on each team, ensure that players each have a turn at taking the draw. If you have several groups of three, you can do best of five with each player rotating to take at least one draw. Encourage players to watch what is happening around them. They should notice what hand the edge battles are and what the other center is trying to do on the draw. Taking in information should help their chances of winning the draw.

3 VS 3 FACE-OFF—OFFENSE AND DEFENSE

Level of Difficulty

Moderate

Minutes

8-10

Players

Full team

Objectives

To help players react one way or another (win or lose) and decide what they should do based on what they see.

Setup

Players set up in a 3 vs 3. One team is on the offensive side of the face-off, and the other team on the defensive side of the face-off. All other players wait outside the blue line. If you have two goalies, you can do this in each end. The coach drops the puck and lets the shift begin from a face-off.

Procedure

After the coach drops the puck, the players work to win the draw. If a team wins the draw offensively, the defensive team must react to what is happening by playing the puck and covering players. Players should be ready for each draw because a defensive-zone draw could lead to a chance to the net for the offensive team. Defense can play offensively if they are lined up on the offensive side, but they should play defense if they are lined up on the defensive side boards or in the middle of the ice. Teams can change the way they line up offensively and work to score a goal. The defensive team must react and line up in a way that minimizes any chances at the net.

Coaching Tips

- Watch how players react to won and lost draws and be ready to make adjustments with them while they wait. Have them watch other players in the game because they will learn from their teammates.
- Encourage defensive players to read the other center and watch how they line up to ensure that no quick-strike offensive chances will be coming against them.

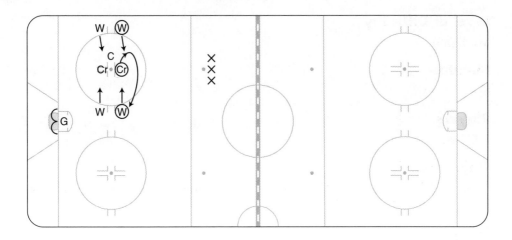

WINNER STAYS

Level of Difficulty
Moderate

Minutes
8-10

Players
Full team

Objectives
To work on winning face-offs in the defensive zone and staying in to focus on beating different players. The goal is to win repeated face-offs.

Setup
Players are in a 1 vs 1 setup in small groups spread out around the ice. One player drops the puck for a face-off between the other two players.

Procedure
This fast-moving game can be played on multiple face-off dots spread out all over the ice. With two players lined up to take the face-off and another player dropping the puck, the face-off will have one winner. The player who successfully pulls the puck back to their side wins the draw. The winner moves to the defensive position and stays there until they get beat. Keep track of who wins the most face-offs in the defensive position and record those numbers for the next time the group plays.

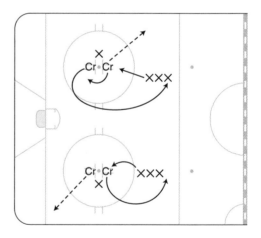

Coaching Tips
- This game will start to show you who should take key face-offs in games.
- Encourage players to try different ways to win the face-off against different players or different-handed (right- or left-handed) players. Encourage players to battle for loose pucks and work to gain possession.

Variation
- This game can also be played 2 vs 2, 3 vs 3, or 5 vs 5 in a scrimmage-type setting with one goalie.

FACE-OFF 3 VS 3—CROSS ICE

Level of Difficulty
Moderate

Minutes
8-10

Players
Full team

Objectives
To work on getting possession and making something happen from possession.

Setup
Divide players into two teams. Three players play against three players from the other team. Place nets across the ice from each other, and have goalies in the nets. The coach has pucks at the middle of the blue line. The coach is involved in the game because they need to drop pucks to restart the game.

Procedure
The coach starts each shift with a face-off. After a team gets possession, they should look to make something happen quickly. The group can work to run a play that they discussed previously while waiting. The game continues until a goal is scored, a goalie freezes the puck, or a new puck is needed. The coach can move the face-off to various areas of the zone to see how players react.

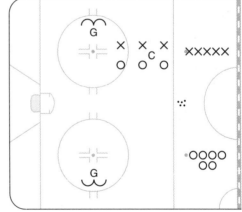

Coaching Tip
- The centers have an advantage in this game, so encourage every player to take the draw and work to communicate what they would like to have happen. Encourage communication among your group of players as well.

Variation
- You can play this game 5 vs 5 in the defensive or offensive zone if you have one goalie, or you can turn this into a game situation.

2 VS 1 FACE-OFF

Level of Difficulty
Easy

Minutes
6-8

Players
Small groups divided up all over the ice or a small group at the end of practice

Objectives
To have the player with support know where the support is. Have the center work to tie up the draw to allow the support to come into the face-off to grab the puck. The center can try to win the draw directly to support as well.

Setup
Have a 1 vs 1 on a face-off dot with one of the players having another player behind or beside them as support. The support player can be on the offensive side of the draw or the defensive side of the draw. The support player can move around from side to side for the player they are supporting.

Procedure
A coach or player drops pucks for the players, who are ready to take a face-off. The center with support must know where their support is and have them help to win the face-off or work to get the puck to them. Each face-off is worth 1 point, and it is a race to 5 points before new players go in.

Coaching Tips
- The center should know before the face-off where their support is for each draw. The more aware they are before the face-off, the better off your team will be in games.
- Have players work on straight speed, hitting the stick first, or tying up the draw to work to get the puck to their support.

Variation
- This game can be played with a support player on both sides of the face-off (offensive and defensive support).

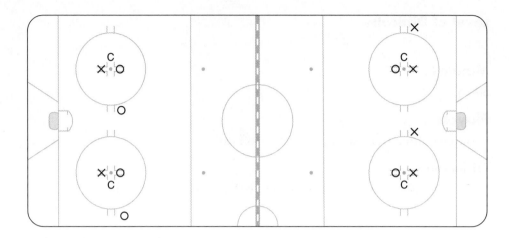

SPEED DRAWS

Level of Difficulty
Easy

Minutes
6-8

Players
Groups of three all over the ice on face-off dots

Objectives
To work on players' straight speed and balance on face-offs.

Setup
A group of three players sets up on a dot. Two players take the draw, and one player drops pucks.

Procedure
The player dropping the puck is in control of the pace of the drill. The two players taking the draw remain set. At the drop, both players try to win the draw quickly. As soon as the two players have their sticks ready again, the third player drops a second puck. After five pucks, the players rotate around.

Coaching Tips
- Encourage players to have a wide base and slide their hands down their sticks a little bit.
- Players should be close to the circle to help with strength on the puck. They need to move quickly and be explosive on draws.

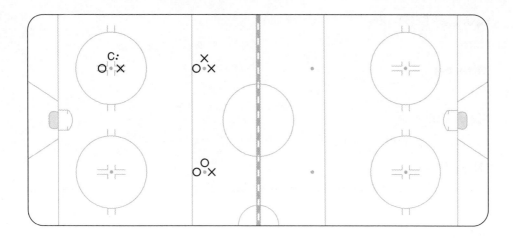

5 VS 5 GAME SIMULATED

Level of Difficulty
Hard

Minutes
8-10

Players:
10 players and one goalie

Objectives
To work on a defensive-zone or offensive-zone face-off and winning possession either way.

Setup
Five offensive players set up for a face-off. Five defensive players are on the defensive side of the draw. A coach drops the puck as a ref would in a game. Each face-off runs for 10 seconds after the draw to allow a play to happen. If the offensive team gets a shot, they get 1 point. If they score, they get 3 points. If the defensive team wins the draw and maintains possession, they get 1 point. If they clear the zone, they get 3 points. If nothing happens on the draw, no points are awarded.

Procedure
When the puck is dropped, the game is on. The offensive team works to gain quick possession of the puck and get it to the net. The defensive team works to win the face-off and quickly get it out of the zone. The group that sets up for the face-off has three face-offs to make something happen before players rotate.

Coaching Tip
- This game is a good way to work on set plays off face-offs for your team offensively and defensively.

Variations
- This game can be changed to simulate various situations in games.
- 5 vs 4—power play vs penalty killers
- 5 vs 3—power play vs penalty killers
- 6 vs 5—end-of-game scenario with the goalie pulled

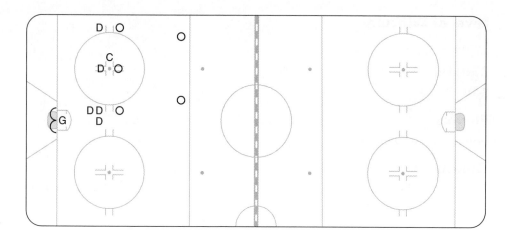

1 VS 5 FACE-OFF

Level of Difficulty
Hard

Minutes
8-10

Players
Full team (half in each end)

Objectives
To work on the defensive-zone face-off, coverage, and plays off a face-off set up in the defensive zone.

Setup
Five defensive players (three forwards and two defenders) line up in the defensive zone. One offensive player takes the draw. The one offensive player tries to win the draw to gain possession and get the puck to the net. The five defensive players must work to get the draw under control and cleanly exit the zone against the pressure of the one offensive player.

Procedure
The puck is dropped in with five defensive players lined up properly for the draw. The one offensive player tries to win the draw and put pressure on the puck. If the defensive team wins the draw, the one offensive player can pressure the puck to force the defensive team to react under pressure. The defensive team should react calmly under the pressure of one player and pass the puck past them to get the puck out of the zone. Every exit the defensive team makes is worth 1 point, and every shot on goal against them is worth 1 point for the offensive player.

Coaching Tips
- Put some pressure on the defensive center to win the draw and eliminate the chance for a shot toward the net.
- If the offensive player wins the draw, all five players do not have to check them right away. The defensive team should roll off the face-off in good positioning to take away space and options for the offensive player.

Variation
- As players get the hang of this, more offensive players can be added in to make this more like a game situation. Slowly work this up to 5 vs 5.

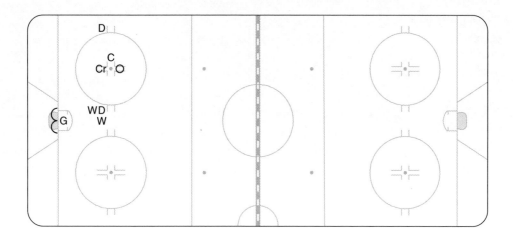

CHAPTER 8

How to Apply to Game-Like Situations

A challenging part of being a coach is taking what you see in games and transferring that concept back to practice to work on it before the next game. One of the best parts of being a coach is seeing your team have success in a game setting from something you worked on in practice. Making this happen consistently is a tough challenge. You must be able to recognize game situations that can be worked on in practice and through small-area games.

VIDEO AS A COACHING TOOL

The ability to recognize areas to work on comes from watching games as well as video of games. As a coach, you will miss situations that happen in a game either because of your point of view from the bench or because your attention was elsewhere. High-level coaches rely extensively on video to ensure that they can accurately break down a game and pass on messages to players. Younger players can benefit from the use of video because they can see the game from a different perspective and, if they are keen, learn from what they see. Video is a great way for players to learn about game situations or see themselves making decisions in game action. They can see options with the puck and may recognize that by making a different decision they could have made things happen easier. Players (young and old) can also use video to confirm that they made the right decision, and everyone in the group may be able to learn from their decision.

The ability to pick up information either from the game or from video will help you be a better coach. Remember that the role of the coach does not concern one game, but rather what you are able to do for the entire season through practice and from game to game to develop your players. The goal for coaches of young players should be to help them see the enjoyment that hockey can bring to their lives and to help them be excited about playing next season. As players get older, the focus can shift to development and ultimately, at the highest levels, to winning. As a coach, your ability to pick up things to work on should follow a plan that you laid out to start the season. You can add topics from the games you have played and apply them to the practice time that you have allotted to your team.

TURNING GAME SITUATIONS INTO FUNCTIONAL WORK

The abundance of information that comes at a coach over the course of a game can be overwhelming at times. The key is to think about what you can do to make the team better at that topic. Through functional work in practice and the use of small-area games, the goal is to see players start to improve in that area as they continue to play games.

Breakouts

Take breakouts as an example of a game-like situation that you can work on in practice before taking it into games. The key to breakouts is puck possession, passing, and support. Without puck possession your team will not have success breaking out of the zone. A player who goes back slowly for the puck is giving away ice to the opposing player who is willing to get to the puck first. The first thing to work on with your group is to get to loose pucks first. You can use a variety of drills that challenge players to work back to the puck to gain possession. They should be able to shoulder check on the way back to the puck to know exactly what is coming at them and where their teammates are as a passing option. When we work with players on this, we call it pressure and support. After players gain possession of the puck, they have to move it to a waiting teammate. By knowing their options with the puck before they get it, they can make earlier and better decisions. After they move the puck, the player receiving the pass must receive it cleanly and continue to advance the puck to make the next play. Other players must support the puck by coming from underneath it so that passing lanes are easy and accessible. When we do this in a practice setting before getting into a game where there is pressure, we allow players to work through the repetition of puck retrieval, passing, pass receiving, puck support, and timing. Communication is also a key part to breaking out of your own zone, so encourage players to yell loudly to each other about exactly what they want to happen with the puck. By working on each individual component, the coach can identify what is going wrong in practice before carrying those concepts into games and struggling again. As each individual area improves, the breakout in a game should start to improve as well. After you have worked on the components in practice, you can begin to put some pressure to them by adding them to small-area games to help prepare players for the game-like situation. You can pick whatever game you believe will help bring out those specific areas. The game does not have to work specifically on breakouts, but it should reinforce the areas of puck possession, passing, and support. Encourage the players off the puck to move to available ice so that the puck carrier always has multiple options with the puck. By reinforcing those key areas, you can help players tie the ideas into their situational play in a game.

Power Plays

Another game situation that you can work on with your team is the power play. Start with the face-off in the offensive zone. If your team wins the draw, they get more time in the offensive zone to try to score. If they lose the first face-off, they must go back and work to break the puck out of your own zone. The power play is a tough concept for younger players because many think they can relax or enjoy an easy shift. The older players realize that the power play is a great opportunity to score and create an offensive advantage.

You can focus on many areas in practice and then build through small-area games before ultimately having power-play chances in games. Passing and puck support are key areas of the power play that you can work on in practice and then expect to see in games. The key is having players pass the puck to teammates in a position where they can handle it and do something with it again quickly. Having options on a breakout coming up the ice and leading into the zone is mandatory on any successful power play because you have more space to work and one or two more players than the other team.

Offensive Setups

In the offensive zone, the setup is based on what you as the coach want to see. The best setups have all five players involved as options for the puck carrier, either one or two passes away. For younger players, this setup can mean that players are in an overload with everyone on the same side of the ice. Older players can set up in a 1-3-1 with a bumper for additional support. Whatever setup you decide to use with your team, you can choose drills to reinforce ideas about how the puck moves in games and what type of pressure your team may see. After working on those concepts in practice, add some small-area games to focus on puck movement and puck support to reinforce the ideas to players. The more they learn about playing without the puck and becoming a passing option, the better off they will be as the game gets faster.

For younger players, practicing with passing and moving off the half wall will prove to be beneficial when they are able to take those skills into games. Having passing options in specific spots will help them to understand where they need to stand in games to become available to get a pass. The give-and-go is a simple way to create movement through puck support and movement. If the passing option is not there, the puck carrier can replace the player on the wall and start again. If they are in an overload position, they should have an option down on the goal line and an option up top at the blue line with a player in the slot.

For older players, working on the power play revolves around having possession of the puck. If they do not have possession, they will not score. They need to work to get the puck back and then move it around quickly to create scoring chances. Their quick puck movement and support will open up lanes to the net where chances can be generated. If players refuse to pass the puck, the power play is not much of an advantage. Encourage players to move the puck quickly and on their teammates' tape in drills and small-area games. Ideally, this skill will carry over into games.

PINPOINTING AREAS FOR IMPROVEMENT

When you are looking to tie situations from games back to practice and then work them back into games, you need to identify the situation and be able to sort out how to work on it with the team in a practice setting. Watching the game with a mindset of seeing what is happening and working out how the team can get better is different from just watching the game. Identifying individual aspects takes practice and is challenging for many coaches. Here are some areas that coaches can analyze in games.

Skating

Is the group skating to their ability? Are they adjusting or reacting to the game at a pace that allows them to stay with the speed of play? Players who are having trouble with skating often either allow the game to come to them and fail to get up in the play or react slowly to ensure they are in a good spot.

Encourage players to push their skating to a level where they react quickly in the game through full strides, confined-space footwork, transitions, or whatever other combination of footwork is necessary.

Passing

Is your team passing on the tape so that a teammate can control it? Are they aware of what hand the other player is, and are they putting the pass into a spot that makes it easier for the next play? Are they passing hard enough that the other team is not intercepting or breaking up the passes to their teammate? You can focus on this area in practice to ensure that players are passing the puck hard enough and that players are receiving the passes that come to them. Coaches can ensure that the players who are receiving the puck have their bottom hand gripped firmly enough that the puck stops when it hits their stick. The blade angle is important because the wrong angle will cause the pass to bounce off the stick. Passing can be worked on with players stationary, in drills, or in small-area games. Passing is an underrated skill that players think they do not need to work on, but they can always benefit by working on passing and pass reception. They can practice backhand passes, backhand receptions, one-touch passes, deceptive passes, changing the angle of their hands to pass, and much more.

Puck Support

Is your team working to become available for good, hard passes? This topic is a key for any team, and it is important in every shift all over the ice—in the defensive zone, in the neutral zone, and in the offensive zone. Players who do not have the puck must realize that they create options for the puck carrier. If they are not moving to available ice, there will be no puck movement.

Timing

Are players without the puck in the right spot at the time when the player with the puck is ready to pass it? This important area builds on puck support; players need to be in a passing lane when the passer is ready to pass the puck. Players are often too far ahead, causing the passing lane to be very small. They should be in a lane that creates a passing angle that allows them to see the puck and the pressure coming at them. This point becomes more important as contact is introduced. If players are in a poor spot to receive a pass, they are more likely to get hit hard. Players should be coming from below the puck in the neutral zone to support the puck with good timing and the correct angle.

Puck Possession

Is your team working to get to loose pucks first to gain possession of the puck for your team? Ultimately, possession starts with face-offs and carries into the game play when your team should be looking to maintain possession as often as possible. Your players should strive to be first to loose pucks. Winning loose-puck battles or 50-50 pucks can go a long way to winning the game. Teams that battle for possession of pucks can be extremely hard to play against.

Puck Protection

After a player has the puck, are they willing to protect the puck and continue to advance it against contact from a checker? Typically, players who have confidence with the puck can maintain possession under pressure and make a play. Players without that confidence are more likely to throw away the puck under pressure. Are players able to feel pressure and maintain their awareness of what is happening around them by scanning the ice? You can add this skill into practice through teaching, drills, and eventually small-area games.

Communication

Is the group communicating in the game to make decision making easier for the player with the puck? Is the communication to the player with the puck clear and easy to understand? Are players talking to each other when they do not have the puck to make the next play easier?

Is the Defense Getting Shots Through From the Point?

This way of creating offense from the back end in a game is something that your team can work on in practice. If this occurrence is a one-time thing in a game, it can be addressed with the player, but if it happens repeatedly, you may need to address it with the team.

Are the Forwards Attacking With Speed Through the Neutral Zone?

If your team is attacking with speed, they will likely create some offense off the rush. If they are not attacking with speed, they will probably have to dump the puck in often in the game if the defensive team has a good gap in the neutral zone. If they are attacking with speed, the group should be able to add layers to the offensive attack by having late players join the rush.

Is the Power Play Functioning the Way You Have Drawn It Up and Worked on It in Practice?

Although your team may not score on the power play, you want them to be in the right spots and moving the puck quick enough to create scoring opportunities. Are they supporting each other on the ice to create multiple options to pass the puck?

Does the Penalty Kill Work the Way You Have Explained It and Worked on It in Practice?

Is your team putting pressure on the puck when they should be? Are players working together when they are down a player? Are they in shooting lanes when opponents are prepared to shoot? Are they getting to loose pucks first and clearing the puck all the way down the ice when they have a chance to do so?

Are the Line Changes at a Length That Allows the Players to Maintain a Fast Pace for the Entire Game?

Are the line changes at the right time in the game to ensure that constant pressure can be placed on the other team? Do the offensive-zone changes allow your players to be fresh against the other team's tired players?

How Is the Team Doing on Face-Offs?

Are they winning the puck clean back, or is every face-off a battle? Is there one player on the other team who is exceptional on face-offs and causing a problem for your team?

You can take all the previously discussed situations from the game and use them in a practice setting before working to apply them in a small-area game. Either through warm-up, transition games, specialty team games, offensive and defensive games, or face-off games, you can use small-area games to help players prepare for that situation when it comes up in a game

> # COACHING TIP
>
> Start slowly with your group and work on the fundamentals of the skill first. This approach allows players to build the confidence they need to use the skill in a game. After players learn the basics of the skill, you can add speed to challenge the players to use the skill and make decisions in drills. As players progress through practice, they will continue to work on the skills at a pace that is closer to that in games.

setting. The repetition in practice and small-area games will help players build confidence in their ability in the situation through constant feedback from the coaches. After the coach explains to players why they are doing something and what options they have in that situation, players should be able to make a decision based on what they see at that moment. Through small-area games and pressure, players' decision making will become quicker and better.

APPROACHES TO REINFORCING A CONCEPT

If players are aware of what they are working on, coaches who are near them in practice have a great chance to reinforce exactly what they want to see. When topics or situations are not being communicated well enough (either coach to player or coach to group), things will begin to break down. The coaching staff can use several approaches to get things back on track when breakdowns occur:

- They can use a teaching approach by explaining things again and working on them in practice time.
- They can take a hard stance by forcing the group to work harder through drill and game selection.
- They can take a light approach by talking about things but not really working on them in drills or small-area games.

How you address the situation will depend on the age of players, the time of year, and what you want to get out of the situation. Having the ability to read your group of players and decide what you need to do comes from experience.

With younger players, taking a teaching approach will allow them to work through drills and small-area games to reinforce areas you are working on. Specific areas can be focused on and worked through. This approach can work well and keep a full team of players involved in practice and the work needed. This type of approach is effective at the start of the season as key areas are being reinforced.

Taking a harder stance is often better for older players who may have come off a bad game or situation and really need to work hard. You can do this by selecting drills and small-area games to reinforce areas you would like to see worked on and improved on. The time of the year may be important here. A hardline approach may be useful early in the season to set the tone with expectations, or it can be used later in the year to send a message that hard work is needed or that they need to prepare for a match against tougher competition. The time in the year and the energy level of the group are relevant topics when planning a harder practice with drills and small-area games.

The light approach may be more appropriate near the end of the season when the team is in the playoffs or is coming off a game with limited time to prepare before the next one. You might address areas of importance but not really work on them in practice. Players should be able to make adjustments from conversations without the work in practice. This approach typically works best with older players who are in their prime competition ages.

Players are typically open to coaching because one of the reasons they are playing the game is to improve. When players are having trouble learning specific areas of the game, your job is to coach them. Players make mistakes, of course, and you as a coach must correct those mistakes. You can spend time talking with your players, and ultimately the goal is to have players not make the same mistake twice.

Whatever your approach is as a coach, the goal is to work to see players improve. Their improvement will happen in practice when you can communicate with them while working through reps of the specific situation. You create the situations through drills and small-area games. Ultimately, players will have an opportunity to shine in matches. By working with players on both individual needs and team needs, you will help them feel that they are getting better. As the season moves on, the players' confidence should increase, and it can be directly tied to what you are doing as a coach in practice. Players should feel confident about their ability to react to each game situation.

CHAPTER 9

Developing Practice Plans From Drills to Small-Area Games

As a skill development coach, I take a different perspective when I look at practice time compared with many other coaches. I look at what skills can be worked on and the drills that can help players become comfortable with those skills. I consider many factors that allow players to maximize their time in practice to see incremental improvements in their game. Developing players' confidence comes from repetition in drills as well as corrective feedback from coaches. Players will take big steps in their development in practice and will get to showcase their development in games.

Motivating players to practice can be a challenge, especially when they are practicing a lot. A coach puts together a practice plan for what they want to accomplish for every practice, but the players often dictate what comes out of that practice. The result can vary among the different age groups because of the factors associated with minor hockey compared with professional hockey. Items to consider when developing practice plans are the schedule leading up to the next game and the plan that will be used to work toward that next game.

Young players will be excited about practice because they will be playing the game they love and will be around their friends who have the same interests they do. As a coach, you should watch the dynamic in the dressing room and see the excitement that comes from players being together. The goal is to take that energy and excitement in the room and transfer it onto the ice so that each player will benefit and develop from the practice. Young players will enjoy the practice because they view the upcoming game as a reward and love the game element.

As players get older, practice is not as interesting or exciting for all players. The players who really want to challenge themselves to play at the highest levels will have no trouble coming to practice and doing what they need to do to get better. A separation will occur when players who enjoy practice will be approached by players who do not enjoy practice as much. Those in the first group will have to decide which way to go. The best way to maintain a positive attitude about practice is to keep players engaged and make sure that the areas you are addressing will show them some direct benefit to their game as an individual (skating, puck skills, shooting, position-specific skills) or as a team (positional play, defensive-zone coverage, power play, neutral-zone regroups). When players feel connected to practice and understand the benefits of drills and teaching, their motivation to practice will remain high, which will ultimately lead to more development for them as well as your team.

In practice, players skate more than they do in a game. They touch the puck more, attempt more passes, receive more passes, and take more shots on goal. Furthermore, players will have more communication with teammates and receive more teaching, more instruction, and more feedback from coaches. The combination of all these areas allows players to develop more confidence leading into games.

> As each player improves, the overall level of your team rises.

SKILLS PRACTICE—DEVELOPMENT PROGRESSION PLAN

I am fortunate to be able to focus on this area almost daily. We get to work with players or teams on specific areas of the game that will have a direct connection to something they can use in their next game.

The difference for me between skills practices and team practices is that I can focus on one topic and really work to develop that topic through progressions and corrective feedback. When planning team practices, coaches often think they need to address multiple topics because practice time is limited. Keep in mind that when planning practice, the more topics you work on, the more topics players have to remember. If you really want something to sink in for the players, streamline the information you give them. As a coach, you can pick drills that work on the same topic in different ways, with more players, or with pressure. The drills can progress through practice to allow players to continue to work on a specific topic. My personal philosophy is to work on skills that are directly transferable from practice to games by working through a sequence of progressions.

Stationary

This phase allows players to learn the movements or understand exactly what we are working on. Players can start to develop confidence in their ability with no pressure of failing. The time spent in this first phase depends on the age of the players, their skill, their ability to understand the concept, and their ability to master the skill. This is where players begin to use the decision-making process because they understand the concepts. If players cannot do things when stationary, they will have trouble doing anything with more speed.

Moving

By adding motion we begin to challenge players with the designated skill. We learn whether players have confidence in the movement or concept, and we allow them to expand their existing skill set. The addition of speed can be at each player's skill level. Some will start slow, and simply moving can be a challenge for them, whereas others will have the skill and be able to add more movement. Keep in mind that the movement can be straight or in different directions based on the skill. By adding movement to a skill like stickhandling, we can start to develop players' vision by having them look over their shoulders while keeping the puck in a good spot.

Speed

As players get the hang of moving in the drills, we start to encourage them to go faster. Ultimately, the player will have to use the skill at game pace with opponents trying to check them, so developing the necessary confidence with speed is important. In a teaching progression, building up to speed will help the skills to stick and allow those skills or concepts to come out in games.

Pressure

Pressure and speed can go hand in hand and can often be used in the same drill as a second option. Adding pressure is a good way to make players go faster. By adding a chaser or otherwise putting players under pressure, you will make the drill or situation more game-like. Players will be forced to move more as they would in a game and should take pride in possession of the puck. You can create situations that include a second puck so that the

COACHING TIP

Occasionally, I discuss with my players whether they want to be a player who plays hockey or a hockey player. Both situations are perfectly fine, but what I try to get players to realize is that depending on which one they want to be, they need to have a certain level of commitment and dedication. To say that you want to be a hockey player requires a lot of effort both on and off the ice. It takes time in practice, time in the gym, time to focus on nutrition, time to rest and recover, and a dedicated focus on school to open up more opportunities and prepare to move forward. Those who really want to be hockey players must have a passion for the process of development. Some players will tell you that they really want to be hockey players, but they are not willing to put in the time or effort to make that happen. Those are the players who get frustrated when things do not happen for them or are surprised when other players have success and they do not. When players can get their thoughts about practice on the same page as their work ethic and attitude about practice, they will see more development and have a better chance to see long-term success.

offensive player stays on offense should they lose possession of the first puck. Alternatively, on a change of possession the defensive player becomes the offensive player, thus increasing the value of the possession.

Game-Simulated Drills

Simulating game situations is an effective way to help players to build confidence in a specific area. They will feel as if they have been there before and can make faster decisions about what to do. Small-area games can connect the topics that were worked on in practice to their use in games.

TEAM PRACTICE—FOCUS ON TEAM NEEDS

The needs of the team will be dictated by the time of the season, and each team will be different based on age, skill level, schedule, and the best use of practice time. Developing effective practice plans is difficult because a lot of time is needed to get a read on what practice should be based on. Factors to consider when developing team practice plans include what happened in recent games, what is coming up in the schedule, what the energy level of the group is, how many players are on the ice, and what messages need to be sent to the players so that they remember topics or concepts.

Differences Between Younger and Older Players

Team practice with younger players can still center on individual development because the game is more about fun and less about the competition or winning. This time is important for developing younger players' passion for the game as well as setting the foundation for their hockey abilities. This is a great opportunity to work on skating, puckhandling, passing, and shooting. Allow players lots of repetition in the drills to build their confidence. Team drills (or bigger drills) can be used to illustrate how the skills will transfer into the games, but the drills should remain simple. Create situations that focus on puck movement and teach players the importance of passing to available teammates. Inevitably, some players will be stronger than others and will have the ability to carry the puck through the other players. By encouraging passing at a young age and strengthening pass reception skills, you will find that executing team systems and puck support will become easier. Build individual skills like shooting with proper technique, which you can develop through instruction and correction of errors. Focus on details such as using a balanced stance, which will lead to more success in shooting. How players hold their stick can make shooting much easier or much harder. If poor technique is not corrected, players will have trouble with proper wrist movements as they continue to develop. The most important aspect of team practice with young players is that they enjoy the game; coaches should see players smiling and having fun. If the players are enjoying the experience, they will want to come back, and by spending time on the ice, they will continue to develop through hard work and planned progressions from the coaches.

As players get older, team practice often focuses on team development, not individual player development. Drills center on what is best for the team, and players are expected to have the skills to complete those drills or execute the system (or structure) the coach is looking for. I am increasingly seeing that the successful teams are dedicating time to player development to break up the routine of regular practice and repeated drills. As a coach, you will set the energy standard for your team. If you can bring life and energy to practice (in whatever way works for you as a coach), you will find that players feed off your enthusiasm. When more is riding on the games with the pressure to win and when practice time becomes limited, you need to find a way to maximize the time in practice to ensure that you are working on the points you want to improve.

Planning for the Unplanned

Keep in mind that despite all your efforts in planning, practice will not go perfectly every day. On some days you will have to throw the practice plan out the window because for whatever reason, it just was not going to work. That is OK, and your ability to adapt and change on the fly will come from experience. Be creative and work to understand how your players are receiving the information you (or your staff) are passing on.

Things to consider when planning team practice:

- What is the most important topic to cover that day?
- What from the previous game did not work that you can address in your practice to correct it? You can even do this with very young players with a topic like passing. If the team did not pass the puck well in the last game, how can you set up drills that will create a clear opportunity to pass the puck?
- Do you have all your players? This issue is more common with older groups because injuries or various situations may take players away from your team. If you only have one goalie, do your drills still allow you to accomplish what you want to accomplish? Players will be less interested right at the start of practice if they know they are shooting on an empty net or targets. I have found it successful to let players know that the drills we will be doing in that end of the ice are not useful for goalies, so we do them on a day when no goalie is available. The drills revolve around taking multiple shots quickly or one-timers with cross-crease passes. When players work on these concepts and get more reps because they do not have to wait for the goalie to get set, they quickly realize days with one goalie can be valuable.
- What topics are working well that you can continue to work to reinforce and build more confidence in?
- Are your players ready for a change in structure or a new concept, or are you continuing to reinforce things they should already know?

PLAN FOR THE END RESULT

When I work with teams and coaches, the most important question I ask is this: "What do you want to have the players work on to get better at?" Often, the answer is something like breakouts. What I do with this information is to suggest that instead of working on breakouts, they work on puck skills, passing, pass receiving, timing, spacing, communication, chips, passing lanes (passing angles), defensive partner support, and partner options. By working on a couple of those components and then combining them, we can see topics like breakouts start to improve as players improve at the individual skills that lead to team success. If players are not confident with the puck or are unable to execute passes, the success of a breakout will be extremely limited. Taking the necessary time with players of any age to work on topics like puck handling, puck protection, and passing and pass receiving with proper technique will yield huge benefits down the road. I am fortunate that I get to watch a lot of practices of both young players and professional players, and I commonly see the youngest players working far ahead of what their skill level allows and professional players working on the finer details that their skill set is well beyond (like backhand receptions). The pro players know that the difference between making it or not making it is so slim that by focusing on the finer details, they can possibly get a small step ahead of someone else. By adding in the finer details at a younger age with a good progression plan, coaches can continue to accelerate the level of player development.

One of the biggest things I try to do when working with teams is to change the way that the coaches view practice in structuring their plans. Rather than focus on practice as a whole and pull out drills to fill the time they have, coaches should view practice in the form of the concepts that can be worked on and create situations where players can execute those concepts. By re-creating concepts in practice and working on them through detailed progressions, you can lead your team through a variety of development opportunities that can translate to success moving forward.

Adding various areas of focus to practice can be something to build on. Some coaches focus on one topic for a day, and some try to incorporate more into a practice plan to ensure that players are getting a variety of drills to work on shooting and scoring. By focusing on these specific areas, you can add skills for your forwards, your defense, and your goalies. Focusing on situations in practice can help prepare players for situations that will come up in games. Here are some examples of situations that come up in practice before games:

- 2 vs 1 situations
- Offensive-zone entries
- Down low plays
- Screens, tips, and redirections
- Defensive-zone net-front play
- Face-offs

ENGAGE PLAYERS TO FUEL GROWTH

To make practice more engaging, consider what you do in your own professional life. If you repeatedly do the same thing, at some point that task will become less interesting. Having young players do the same practice repeatedly will ultimately lead to them becoming disengaged because they will not feel like the practice is benefitting them. If at any point the players feel as though they can predict the day or drill that will be used, you risk the chance of them going on autopilot for that practice (or drill) and potentially missing an opportunity to improve in a small area of the drill. The goal for any coach should be to continue to challenge players to improve over the course of the season. They can do this by improving their individual skills, by understanding team concepts, or by executing team tactics. If I use a drill a second time with a group or a team, I always have a purpose. The purpose could simply be that over time, their skills have become better and they can now execute that specific drill at a higher level. Passing and pass receiving can improve through better timing and creating better lanes through improved skating or improved puckhandling skills. I may want to illustrate a finer point in the drill that was not explained the first time through because they needed to understand the skeleton of the drill before the details were added. If you explain this in a way that helps the players understand the progression, you will immediately see their continued engagement.

Drills are done for a reason and should follow some progression from the previous drill to produce an effective practice for players of any age.

> Good skating leads to better puck skill. Good puck skills lead to better passing.
> Good passing leads to good shooting. Bad passing leads to no shots.

If players have trouble with balance in their skating, they will have trouble with puckhandling, which leads to less accuracy in passing and lower quality shots on goal. The time spent in building skill is worth it when you are available to help players get the most out of their ice time. When players come to an environment knowing that they will benefit by being there, they will be excited. The following are some ways to keep players engaged in practice.

Have Options

Have a variety of drills to work on the same topic and rotate the drills so that the players are doing something different from practice to practice. Likewise, have options or progressions for the drills so that the next time the players perform them, they are doing something different.

Be Specific

Identify specific areas in drills for each position to focus on. For example, a simple offensive attack option drill can have details within it for each positional player. By giving each position something specific to think about, you can make players more accountable to the drill.

- **Defense**—make a good first pass, get up in the play, be an option on the rush, communicate, shoot the puck quickly, limit stickhandles before you shoot.
- **Forwards**—time the support, attack with speed, support the puck on the rush, make good decisions to get the puck to the net, release the puck quickly, change the angle of the shot, handle the rim clean, pass the puck hard, identify what hand the shooter is, and put the pass on the tape.
- **Goalie**—stop the puck, control the rebound, and battle on second chances.

Connect Topics

Work to tie in things from the games that your team needs to improve on or things you want your team to be able to do and have drills that relate to the topics. This approach will help you as a coach see whether players are improving in those areas. Sometimes when working on a drill, players will not realize they are working on a bigger concept. I used this tactic when working with our provincial team at a Top 40 evaluation before we got down to the final roster for Team Manitoba. Through detailed discussions with the team coaches and provincial directors, we came up with a game plan that we wanted to execute with the final team. I then took their ideas and put together drills and small-area games that would show us which players could think the way we wanted or execute the areas we wanted to develop. Later, when the team was formed and the teaching of structure was implemented, coaches and players were able to relate back to drills and games that they did before and say, "Remember when we did that drill—it was a lead-in to this concept."

Plan by Numbers

Plan drills and games that are effective for the number of players you have on the ice. Even great drills can lose their effectiveness if the number of players to execute the drill is not right. Players will become fatigued quickly, and the drill will lose its effectiveness. In the event that the drill is important in the progression of the practice plan, you can have coaches jump into the drill to provide a couple of extra bodies. Alternatively, you can simply shorten the duration of the drill to allow players to get the instruction and concepts and keep the practice moving forward.

Develop Goaltenders

Think about goaltender development as part of your practice. This area is often overlooked as teams run through their drill lineup for the practice. But this activity plays a huge part in the development of your goalie as well as the engagement of the goalie in practice. Think about the shots your goalie will be facing and plan drills that do not have the same shots in consecutive drills. For example, if a warm-up drill is used and the shot is from the outside lane (as it is in most warm-up drills), the second drill should not be the same shot from the outside lane unless there is some change to the surrounding of the shot. By changing the shot or the movement of the goalie in drills so that they get to work on something different, you will be including your goalie in practice rather than just having them stop pucks.

Keep Lines Moving

Manage the length of the lines in practice by using drills that have multiple players going. Players lose interest in practice if they are standing and waiting. Use your assistant coaches to run the same drill from the other side or other end. The goal in practice is to have players doing more and waiting less.

Manage the Players

If the activity does not distract from the drill, have the waiting players work with a puck so that they stay engaged. Give them three or four things to work on with their time in line. This does not have to be done all the time because there is value in watching other players perform the drill and learning from them, but increasing puck time in practice can be especially helpful for teams or players who lack confidence with the puck.

Manage the Ice

Manage the ice and use it as best you can. Often with youth practice, teams have one goalie and think that they need to run a drill in one end, so every shot is on the goalie. Many drills can be done to work on skills such as stick-handling, puck protection, passing, and shooting (without a goalie) while also using the space at the other end. If you have a full group, dividing the ice into different areas is a good way to limit waiting time and encourage more movement. Think about a layout in which you can do three drills—one in each end zone and one in the neutral zone. The same drill can be used in each end zone (from the opposite side), and the neutral-zone drill can be on a related topic. This setup saves time in switching sides, but you may have to be aware of the moving of the cones or tires depending on the drill because the area will be used repeatedly. Using this setup, players need to remember only two drills but can work in three stations.

Tie It Together

Connect small-area games to your practice plan to build from practicing drills to competitive situations. Players at all levels from beginner to pro love the opportunity to be creative and competitive in a game setting. In addition, you will be able to see whether the players can apply the topics you worked on in practice into games. You can manage shift length and the number of players in the game to ensure that everybody is active with limited waiting time. If necessary, have multiple small-area games going on at the same time to ensure that you are using the ice effectively.

Use the Coaches

Use all your coaches on the ice to communicate with players and keep them focused. Players may find ways to drift in practice, but if coaches around them are talking to them, they will likely stay dialed in. This dialogue can be as simple as asking, "Do you understand the drill?" Or the conversation can be more specific such as by saying, "In this next rep, identify where the pressure is coming from." The coach can stay close to the player and follow up to receive the answer. Having more communication with coaches in a practice will help players recognize that they are getting the attention they need. If coaches do not talk to players, the players are more likely to lose focus or miss the finer details of the drills they are working on.

Ultimately, at the end of the season the goal for players is to be better than they were at the start of the season. Much of that progress can come from the coach's planning of practice. Players will handle the puck much more in practice than they will in games, they will get more shots in practice than they will in games, but they will often not enjoy practice as much as the games, especially at a young age. The challenge for the coach is to motivate players through practice to be their best in games. This result comes from effective planning, consistent feedback and reinforcement, consistent progressions, and challenging players to expand their existing skill sets. What players take out of the season will be influenced by the coach's use of practice time leading into games to continue to build throughout the season.

USE PRACTICE PLANS

The following practice plans allow coaches to work on specific skills and use games at both the start and end of practice. These practices are based on ice times being 60 minutes in duration with a group of 12 to 15 players and at least one goalie. The goals for practice are to build on the previous drills and allow players to build on specific skill sets.

Using a warm-up small-area game at the start of practice is helpful when your group or team needs it. I find this approach most effective when you have worked on a skill and want to come back to it in a different way. A topic like stickhandling is a good area to focus on in a small-area game. A warm-up small-area game can also be effective if you are watching players before practice and think that they are not prepared to work. A game can boost the group at the start of practice and get them going.

The detailed practices are designed to be run during the season for a group of players. These practices are not for a playoff situation, but the drills can be used for any level of player and can be modified by adding more passes or another shot to make them more difficult. You can make the drills easier by removing passing and having a player handle the puck, and you can shorten them to meet the skating needs of the group.

SAMPLE 45-MINUTE PRACTICE PLAN #1

Activity	Description	Objectives and key points
Warm-Up Skate	This activity gets players on the ice. One-foot edges, two-foot edges, and stickhandling can be used in the three or four laps around the ice. Players should not shoot during the warm-up skate.	For an effective warm-up skate, give players something to work on that either will come up later in practice or is a review.
Your Favorite Passing Drill	Have players focus on making flat passes and stopping the puck when it hits their stick.	Players should be able to receive the pass and not allow it to go behind their hips.
Your Favorite Angling Drill	Have players focus on stick position and body position.	Focus on skating to help with angling. Ensure players are comfortable on their edges to put themselves in good spots on the ice.
Your Favorite 1 vs 1 Half-Ice Drill	Work on defensive side positioning to allow D to stay between offensive player and net.	Keep working on angling with good body and stick position.
Small-Area Game: 3 vs 3 Angle	Players should be able to steer their offensive counterparts and force them into an area where they want them to go and to move the puck where there is defensive support.	This is a good cross-ice game that allows players to use angles.

SAMPLE 45-MINUTE PRACTICE PLAN #2

Activity	Description	Objectives and key points
Warm-Up Skate	Players skate laps around the ice, working on various skills.	Players should focus on something specific, like edge acceleration, forward stride extension, backward stride extension, etc.
Your Favorite Stickhandling Drill	Have players focus on having eyes up and making contact between the puck and blade.	The puck should be in the middle of the blade for better control.
Small-Area Game: Neutral-Zone Chaos — Stickhandling	This game creates many things for players to process. As the puck carriers move, they navigate around other players, some moving and some stationary.	Have players focus on moving, having eyes up, and moving away from other players.
Your Favorite Warm-Up Shooting Drill	Have players focus on hitting the net and shooting hard.	When players are receiving passes, have them focus on stopping the puck and not letting it bounce off their stick.

(continued)

SAMPLE 45-MINUTE PRACTICE PLAN #2 (continued)

Activity	Description	Objectives and key points
Small-Area Game: Slot Box Game	This game creates quick plays around the net. Players must move the puck and get open, or shoot and collapse to the rebound.	Players who are open receive the puck from the coach to start. New pucks come in when the puck is pushed outside the box, is scored, or is frozen by the goalie.
Small-Area Game: 3 vs 3 Cross Ice	This is a great game to encourage players to stay on the puck and make quick decisions. Transitions are fast and the shifts should be short.	Encourage players to put the defensive team into tough spots by working to move the puck quickly and jump to the net. Encourage the defensive team to keep body position and work to transition the puck quickly, changing the offensive team to the defensive team.

SAMPLE 60-MINUTE PRACTICE PLAN #1

Activity	Description	Objectives and key points
Warm-Up Skate	Players skate laps around the ice, working on various skills.	Encourage players to work on areas they need to improve.
Your Favorite Edge Skating Drill	Have players focus on balance and gliding.	Players should focus on keeping weight over their skates.
Small-Area Game: 1 vs 1 to Dot Line	Have offensive players focus on good use of edges and defensive players focus on moving their feet to prevent the offensive player from getting to the dot line.	This will start to build up the intensity of the practice. Have players focus on executing without taking penalties.
Your Favorite Shooting Drill	This drill should either allow players to have multiple shots or allow multiple players to shoot.	Encourage players to shoot the puck hard and to good spots.

(continued)

SAMPLE 60-MINUTE PRACTICE PLAN #1 *(continued)*

Activity	Description	Objectives and key points
Small-Area Game: 1 vs 1, 2 vs 2, 3 vs 3	Have players focus on reading the play and jumping to support the puck. After players pass the puck, they should move to get it back.	This is a great drill for spatial awareness. Players must recognize where pressure is coming from and where support is coming from. Encourage players to use position before possession on loose pucks.
Small-Area Game: Neutral-Zone Two-Puck Game	Have players work to score goals while defending their own net. They should make reads about when to leave their net and go to help offensively.	This game is about awareness from all players in each shift. Players must locate their puck and recognize the other team's situation. Whether they are on offense or defense will depend on what is happening in each shift.

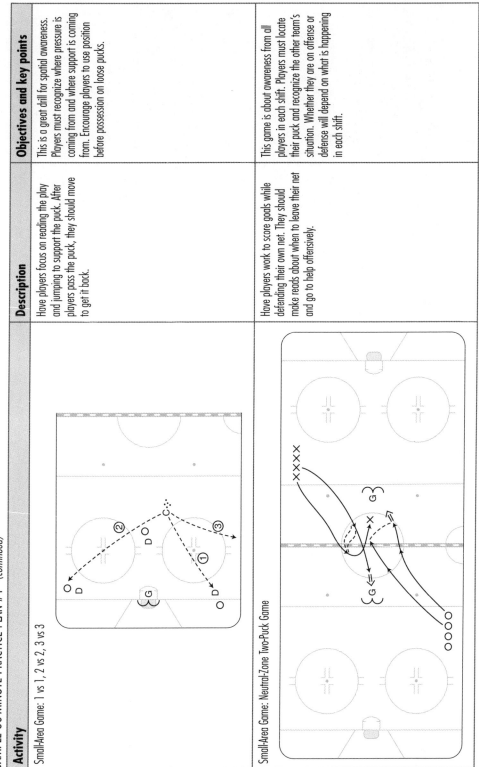

SAMPLE 60-MINUTE PRACTICE PLAN #2

Activity	Description	Objectives and key points
Warm-Up Skate	Players skate laps around the ice, working on various skills.	Use this time to teach or give players more reps of something specific they have done before.
Small-Area Game: Passing for Points	In this game, players need passing options to score points. The players without the puck are more important than the player with the puck. Players pass the puck and then move to get it back.	This is a great game to show that the players without the puck are more important in the game. The player with the puck needs a passing option. If the players without the puck don't move, there won't be a passing option.
Your Favorite Passing and Shooting Drill	This should challenge the players to execute. Players should make a couple of good passes, and there can be multiple shots if needed.	Have players focus on putting passes in good spots so the shooter can shoot. Encourage players to hit the net when shooting.
Your Favorite Drill With 2 Vs 1 With a Second Puck to the Net	This challenges the defender to make a decision to try to stop the 2 vs 1. Offensively, players try to score with an early pass, late pass, or shot.	By adding a second puck to the net, players are forced to stop in front of the net and battle for loose pucks.

(continued)

SAMPLE 60-MINUTE PRACTICE PLAN #2 *(continued)*

Activity	Description	Objectives and key points
Small-Area Game: 2 vs 1 Box Game	This is a simple 2 vs 1 puck movement game.	The game should be played with the mindset to move the puck quickly and then move to get the puck back.
Small-Area Game: Neutral-Zone Two-Puck Game	Players should focus on stick position and denying clear passing lanes.	Encourage players to have their head on a swivel and know where they are moving the puck before they get it.

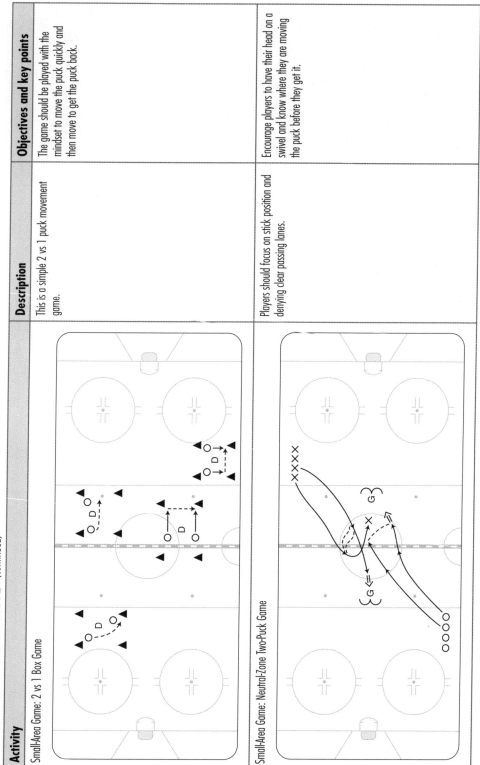

SAMPLE 90-MINUTE PRACTICE PLAN #1

Activity	Description	Objectives and key points
Warm-Up Skate	Players skate laps around the ice, working on various skills.	Give players extra reps on something specific.
Your Favorite Stickhandling Warm-Up Drill	Players should have to work to move and react to different positions.	This is a great chance for players to work on keeping their eyes up and scanning the ice.
Your Favorite Shooting Drill as a Warm-Up for Your Goalies	This activity is primarily a warm-up for your goalies.	Goalies should work to recognize shoot options and read plays before they happen.
Small-Area Game: Three-Zone Scrimmage	This is a game of puck movement and communication. Players must move the puck from the defensive zone up to the offensive zone to work to try to score. A time limit can be placed for three shifts so players play in all three zones.	Encourage players to call loud, as everyone will be calling for pucks. Make good passes, as there will be two pucks used for this game.
Stations	Divide the ice into three zones and run three drills.	By dividing up the group into thirds, players will get more reps.
1 (End Zone)	Shooting and scoring with point shots.	This re-creates game situations and helps to prepare players for different moments.
2 (Neutral Zone)	Pass reception and symmetry skills (forehand and backhand).	This creates opportunities for players to use their forehand and backhand to give and receive passes.

(continued)

SAMPLE 90-MINUTE PRACTICE PLAN #1 *(continued)*

Activity		Description	Objectives and key points
3 (End Zone)		Plays off the rush with pucks to the net. Use both sides of the ice with shots and plays coming to the net either off a shot, a pass and a shot, a deflection, or a shot and a rebound.	This re-creates game situations and helps to prepare players for different scenarios.
Small-Area Game: 3 vs 3 Cross Ice		This game is fast with puck movement and will challenge players to react quickly. They should work to keep defensive side position and transition the puck quickly from defense to offense.	Encourage players to move the puck and then move to get open, as they are always an option to get the puck back once they move it.
Small-Area Game: Add a Player		This game encourages players to think about adding players for a short power play if they can complete passes successfully. Pass to the line and get a pass back to add a player for your team.	Players don't need to add a player to score. If there is an opportunity to score, go ahead and score.

SAMPLE 90-MINUTE PRACTICE PLAN #2

Activity	Description	Objectives and key points
Warm-Up Skate	Players skate laps around the ice, working on various skills.	This is a chance for extra reps on something specific.
Your Favorite Stickhandling Warm-Up	This is an opportunity for players to get a puck on their stick to work on building confidence.	Encourage players to handle the puck with the puck in the middle of the blade, hands roughly shoulder-width apart, and the puck moving flat.
Small-Area Game: Box Warm-Up	Players work to move through the cones with another player chasing them.	Encourage the lead players to be creative in how they move through the four tires or cones. They should be trying to lose the second player.
Your Favorite Warm-Up Drill With Stickhandling, Passing, and Shooting	This should be game-simulated and challenging to execute.	Players should make good passes to a shooter, who works to receive the pass and quickly works to get the puck to the net.
Your Favorite Angling Drill to Teach Angling	Players should think about a simple angle where they can get their body in the correct lane.	This is meant to help players steer other players where they want them to go. Work on stick position and body position to take away space, eventually going shoulder to shoulder.

(continued)

SAMPLE 90-MINUTE PRACTICE PLAN #2 *(continued)*

Activity		Description	Objectives and key points
Your Favorite Competitive Angling Drill		This is meant to be game-like. Encourage the offensive player to work to get to the net. Encourage the defensive player to stop them from getting to the net.	If players are continually getting beat in the angling drills, this shows they need to work on skating.
Small-Area Game: 1 vs 1 With Help Coming		Defensive players should recognize that they have a player behind them and steer the offensive player into the waiting player.	The defensive player coming to help should communicate to the defensive player close to the puck to help them break up possession of the puck.
Small-Area Game: Two Net—Read the Play		This is a quick game that allows for offensive chances to be created through puck movement. Players must react and can score on either net when there is a chance to score.	Players should work to create deception to keep the defensive team guessing where they are going.

(continued)

SAMPLE 90-MINUTE PRACTICE PLAN #2 *(continued)*

Activity		Description	Objectives and key points
Small-Area Game: Pass to Coach		This game promotes puck movement and players continually moving to get open. Teams will pass to a coach to go from defense to offense. Coaches should look to create an offensive chance off the transition.	Players should communicate to the coach if they are available so the coach knows where to move the puck.

ABOUT THE AUTHOR

DAVE CAMERON is the head coach and program director of Jets Hockey Development, a skating and skills coach for Manitoba Moose, and a development coach for Team Canada (both the men's and women's teams). Also a Hockey Canada skills consultant, he has more than 20 years of experience coaching players of all levels: professionals (NHL, AHL, and ECHL), college athletes, and young athletes just learning to play the game. He has helped many players achieve their goals, including being selected in the WHL Bantam Draft, making the jump to the NCAA, being selected in the NHL Entry Draft, and winning the Stanley Cup. Cameron specializes in individual skill development such as power skating, shooting, stickhandling, passing, and position-specific skills. He believes that confidence is built from practice and players can continue to get better through detailed work in specific areas.

Cameron played minor hockey in the Winnipeg area before moving on to the WHL, where he was drafted by the Pittsburgh Penguins in 1998 (third round, 80th overall). He returned to Winnipeg to attend the University of Manitoba, where he obtained a degree in kinesiology before starting his coaching career.